Christina Sinclair Bremner

Education of girls and women in Great Britain

Christina Sinclair Bremner

Education of girls and women in Great Britain

ISBN/EAN: 9783337215361

Printed in Europe, USA, Canada, Australia, Japan

Cover: Foto ©Andreas Hilbeck / pixelio.de

More available books at **www.hansebooks.com**

EDUCATION

OF

GIRLS AND WOMEN

IN GREAT BRITAIN

EDUCATION

OF

GIRLS AND WOMEN

IN GREAT BRITAIN

BY

C. S. BREMNER

WITH A PREFACE BY MISS E. P. HUGHES.

LONDON

SWAN SONNENSCHEIN & CO., LIM.

1897

PREFACE

In tracing the history of any movement, the rate of development at different periods varies strikingly. There may be no growth for a long time; occasionally the tide of progress may appear even to flow back; the spirit of a great reform dies out, and the customs and traditions which have grown up around that reform become a dead weight to hamper progress. Then faint signs of life are to be seen by those who are on the watch, half-hearted protests against traditions, here and there revolts quickly quelled, and some discontent. These are promises of future life and vigour. Suddenly the scene is changed, or rather, it appears to be sudden to the casual observer; it is but the ending of a series of events to those who have watched carefully. We have an outburst of Utopian schemes, many brave beginnings, and many failures. All seems chaos for the time being; currents cross and re-cross; the eternal struggle between the conservative element and the progressive element in humanity is intensified. Gradually out of disorder comes order and rest. But the world is not as it was: the trend of progress is altered; new forces have probably come into operation.

What is true of other aspects of history, is true also of the educational aspect. The latter half of this

century has seen great changes, some of them revolutionary, in the education of the British people. It has
also seen the beginning of still greater changes. Fifty
years ago there was much stagnation. To-day there is
much life, some bewilderment, and what appears to
many to be an ever-increasing chaos. A large number
of educational problems are being formulated, and many
of them must, from the necessity of the case, be solved
quickly, either badly, indifferently, or well. Time will
possibly provide a solution for some of them without our
actual interference; but the majority require careful
thought and conscious effort, if they are to be solved
satisfactorily. A wide knowledge of the educational
state of the country, together with some knowledge of
that which preceded the present state of affairs, will be
of great use in such a momentous period as the present.
Miss Bremner has given us a valuable contribution
towards such knowledge, for which she deserves the
gratitude of all those whose responsible duty it will be
to mould the future of our educational development.
Only those who have for some special purpose attempted
to collect information on the state of education in Great
Britain can appreciate the time, care, and patience which
the writing of such a book as this entails.

Change has been visible in every sphere of education;
it has been most strongly marked in the Secondary
Education of girls and women. In Elementary Education, both in the immediate past and in the present,
there has been no considerable difference between the
education of girls and that of boys, nor between the
education of men and women teachers. In Secondary
Education, the difference in both spheres has been very

marked in the past, and is still considerable; as a result, there is probably less contact between the men and women teachers engaged in Secondary Education than between those engaged in Elementary Education. Partly as a result of this isolation, the development of Secondary Education for girls in England has been of a somewhat special kind, and has special interest for those who are studying the subject. Lately an increasing number of foreigners have visited England for the purpose of seeing our educational establishments. The foreigner who comes to study English education deserves our pity. Many are the difficulties which lie before him. In Elementary Education he has to comprehend two different schemes working concurrently all over the kingdom, Voluntary and Board schools. When he has surmounted this difficulty, and enters the field of Secondary Education, despair may well seize both his instructor and himself. Many secondary teachers in England know little of the educational life outside their own special sphere. What does a High School mistress usually know of the education given at this present moment at Winchester? How far can an assistant master from one of our great public schools describe accurately how life goes on in one of our private commercial schools? It is very difficult for the intelligent foreigner to get information, and even difficult to see the real connection between the facts which he collects. Thanks to this book, a foreigner can for the future obtain easily some insight into the education of girls and women in Britain.

It has been said, with much truth, that the members of a civilized community are so closely linked to one

another that no section can progress safely far beyond
the rest of the community.   In other words, it seems to
be true that safe and permanent progress is only possible
when the rear guard and the advance guard are connected by intermediate sections, all in touch one with
the other.   If this be true, the education of the less
educated half of the nation, girls and women, must
have a special interest.   If the pace of the rear guard
affects the pace of the advance guard, it is everybody's
interest to see that the pace of the rear guard be
quickened.   To attain this end, it might be well worth
while to divide the ancient educational endowments, at
one time enjoyed by boys only, between boys and girls.
If we are believers in that greatest of educators, the life
of the home, it is better to spend a little less money on
boys' education, and help the girls, rather than doom
the boys to live in homes governed by badly educated
mothers and wives.   The education of girls is not
merely a woman's question—thoughtful men have never
so regarded it.   It is a human question, one that concerns every one.   This book, although it deals only
with the education of girls and women, should therefore
be studied by all those who are interested in education.

Just at the present moment Secondary Education in
England requires more consideration than Elementary
Education : the latter is organized, the former is not.
It is a truism that organization gives enormous power.
A constant, wide, ever-deepening stream of state-aid and
rate-aid is passing to the latter; only a tiny streamlet
to the former.   Already it is not an uncommon sight to
come across an elementary school in better buildings,
and better equipped, than a secondary school in the

same town. We are so accustomed to the fact that our Education Department only concerns itself with Elementary Education, that we may fail to realize how Secondary Education is affected by it. To many of us it is a fact of the profoundest significance that political enfranchisement has come to the working-man in England before educational enfranchisement, and the educational results for the time being may be serious. Can we expect the average man who has never enjoyed the benefits of Secondary Education, to realize its enormous value to the nation? It is difficult at present to show its value, because our Secondary Education has been largely a class education, and as such, its national value cannot easily be demonstrated to a democracy. When Secondary Education is given in England to those clever boys and girls from our elementary schools, who can really utilise it, it will then be comparatively easy to show its national importance; but until that time it is placed at a serious disadvantage. Yet it is obviously of the greatest importance to protect most carefully our secondary schools and universities. They are the depositories of the traditions, the culture, and the learning of the past, and are therefore of unique importance. But in order to protect wisely we must understand, and know something about, Secondary Education. This work on the education of girls and women is of considerable value, in that it gives us a fairly complete picture of a part of the Secondary Education of the British Isles.

Every country has, no doubt, its special contribution to make to the education of the world. The British Empire, with its enormous colonies and dependencies in every continent and in every climate, with their widely-different forms of government, has probably for its special educational mission to keep awake a healthy dread of over-centralization in matters educational ; a strong belief in home rule in education ; a firm faith in liberty—liberty of conscience, freedom of method, room for individuality, development, and self-government. If this is the British educational gospel, it is one worth preaching. During the last half-century a large number of secondary schools for girls have sprung up in England. It is interesting to note that on the whole they have been true to English traditions. Our girls' High Schools are not mere copies of the boys' Grammar Schools ; there is differentiation among them, and considerable individuality. Women secondary teachers, considering their disadvantages, have taken their full share in developing education in England.

That educational progress, which has been so marked in England, has also been taking place in other civilized countries ; but in the higher education of girls and women England at the present moment probably stands first. Our progress in this department has been exceptionally rapid, and is probably due largely to the unusual wisdom of the pioneers of the movement. Time has already robbed us of many of that little band of earnest men and women who initiated the movement in England ; but some are, fortunately, still with us. When the time comes to write a history of English education in the nineteenth century, it will be a very bright page that will record the first steps taken in obtaining a higher education for girls and women. Our pioneers toiled unceasingly ; they did more, they waited patiently till times were ripe. They aroused no unnecessary friction ; slowly and surely they won a victory, with results so great that we can at present only dimly guess at them. Now that a younger generation of women are coming to the front to face the new problems of the day, it is exceedingly appropriate that we should look back to those early days. In this book some insight is given us into these first stages of progress, which must have an intense interest for those who are at present beginning to reap the harvest which that pioneer band sowed in great faith and in much anxiety.

There are probably at least four classes of persons who will find an interest in this book :—

(1) British teachers of all kinds, who will be enabled by its means to get a fair survey of the education of the British Isles. That such information is necessary can be doubted by no one who takes the trouble to find out how far the ordinary teacher realizes the differences existing between the various systems of education in England, Scotland, Ireland, and Wales.

(2) Our fellow-teachers in other parts of the British Empire. It is a great loss to the Empire, politically and educationally, that its teachers know so little of the state of education in the different countries which make up that Empire. An Englishwoman has now made it easy for our fellow-teachers to understand a good deal about the present state of Secondary Education for girls in the home country. It is much to be desired that Colonial teachers would issue companion volumes, giving us information about Colonial education. Blue Books are not generally considered to be very

interesting by the average teacher; but the facts to be found in them, enlivened and made graphic by personal experience, are often of the very greatest interest.

(3) Foreigners who desire to understand the present state of English education.

(4) And finally, all those interested in educational progress—parents, teachers, politicians, and social reformers.

Behind us lie the gallant efforts of our pioneer women; around us, the surging chaos of to-day's problems; before us, difficulties many and great. It is of the utmost importance at the present moment for us to clearly realize that the future is largely in our hands; and, in order to build for that future a satisfactory structure, we must know the present, and understand something of the past. Miss Bremner's survey has come at a most opportune moment, and is likely to stimulate considerably the ever-growing interest in education, which is one of the most marked features of our time.

E. P. HUGHES.

AUTHOR'S PREFACE

THIS little book is a rather late outcome of the International Congress of Education held at Chicago in 1893. Some of our American sisters (the National Council of Women, U.S.A.) conceived the brilliant idea of publishing a whole set of reports dealing with the education of girls and women in all civilized countries. Lady Henry Somerset and Miss Frances Willard, whose interest in what affects the well-being of their sex is well known, asked me to undertake education in Great Britain; and it is to this circumstance that this book owes its existence. I sought diligently for such a book as this, failed to find it, was assured by the publishers whom I consulted that such books do not pay, and are therefore not written, and finally sat down to the lengthy undertaking of collecting the facts myself. When it was finished, the American sisters had no funds wherewith to publish it. I sought the advice of Miss E. P. Hughes, of Cambridge, and of an English publisher, rewrote my work since it was now for the English market and required enlargement. I mention these circumstances because they have laid me under heavy obligations to the many persons who have supplied me with information. I had to appeal to them twice for facts, figures, dates.

In especial I have to thank for their ready help and courtesy, officials of the Education Department, of the

Science and Art Department, and Charity Commission; the heads of colleges, schools, boards, and institutions named in this book, who almost all helped me in every possible way; especially Mr. G. W. Alexander, Clerk to the School Board for Glasgow, and Miss Jane Galloway, of Queen Margaret College, Glasgow, who have furnished the Second Part, dealing with Scottish education; Miss Hughes for the Preface and much excellent advice. My helpers are of course in no way responsible for my opinions, inferences, and deductions.

Unfortunately we have been unable to obtain an account of education in Ireland on the same conditions as the Scottish section is supplied: mere devotion to education. If another edition of this book were called for, the omission might be rectified.

It is too much to expect that a book of this kind should be free of error. I shall esteem it a favour if all errors are pointed out to me by readers, so that I may be able to correct them, if the opportunity present itself.

During my visits to colleges and schools I was over and over again struck by the isolation in which women teachers work. Many able and accomplished women know little of the world of education outside the corner of the vineyard which engrosses their attention. Should this book help to bridge that isolation, I shall be well satisfied.

C. S. BREMNER.

March, 1897.

CONTENTS

Education of Girls and Women

IN GREAT BRITAIN

INTRODUCTORY

THE education of girls and women remained entirely in the hands of the Church up to the time of the Reformation. For a long period the Church controlled the education of boys, although gradually a lay element was introduced. Thus the Chantry schools, which existed in cathedral towns, were partly managed by the laity. Towns were rising apart from monasteries, whose wealth, influence, and ever-widening liberties had to be reckoned with; Franciscans and Dominicans visited them and helped on the education of the young. Grammar schools were multiplying. When Eton was founded in 1441 there already existed eight; by the beginning of the sixteenth century their number was very considerable, and at the end of James I.'s reign there were probably more than 300.

Moreover, the universities were another power rising to a position of great importance. Excluding hostels, Oxford has now 23 colleges; 15 of these were in existence in 1539, the date of the final dissolution of the

B

monasteries.   The quarrel between regulars and seculars is well known ; occasionally a new college was founded by a bishop as a practical protest against the narrowness of monastic learning.   Cambridge, of more recent date than Oxford, has seventeen colleges ; thirteen were in existence in 1539.

The consideration of the above facts, and the knowledge that for girls there existed absolutely no organised education outside the nunnery schools, show us that the destruction of the monasteries affected the sexes differently.   The Dissolution found women quite unprepared, and dealt their education such a severe blow, that it is no exaggeration to say it passed under a cloud for 300 years.   Boys lost something by the destruction of the monasteries ; girls lost everything. The latter were not prepared to go to the new seats of learning, even had these been prepared to receive them.

It is true that monastic life was decaying, becoming more and more divorced from the solid interests of life.   The nuns especially were immersed in religious routine ; they were landing themselves in one of life's backwaters.   Important boarding-schools were attached to some of the nunneries, where the daughters of gentle people received what then passed for a good education. Day schools would also seem to have been conducted at some nunneries, notably the Convent of St. Helen, in Bishopsgate, and that of St. Mary, Kilburn.

According to the Benedictine rule children were taught between prime and tierce, probably 5 to 8 a.m.

Nunneries received people of different social conditions, and it may well have been that wealthy convents conducted boarding-schools, attended by the daughters of the nobility, whilst the poorer ones had merely day schools attached.

The Church gave great honour to the professed ; they and their pupils were addressed as "madame" or "ladye." Chaucer's miller's wife had been "i-fostyrd in a nonnerye, and whom no one durst call but madame." The nuns enjoyed the esteem and affection of their contemporaries. The Pilgrimage of Grace in 1536 had amongst its objects the restoration of the nunneries. In the eighth century the Bishop of Sherbourne wrote the "Praise of Virgins," telling them that even in outward appearance they surpass their married sisters. "Virginity is of gold, chastity is of silver, marriage is of brass." In one place he addresses the nuns as "Flowers of the Church, sisters of monastic life, scholarly pupils, pearls of Christ, jewels of Paradise, and sharers of the Eternal Home." *

Nor was Ealdhelm the only one impressed with the beauty of the nun's life. Boniface so admired the character and ability of English nuns as rulers that he took many of them abroad to help in the work of organizing Germany for the Church of Rome. In a word, the Church found an outlet for women's abilities, and stamped their labour with its high approval.

* See Miss ECKENSTEIN's able work, *Woman under Monasticism*.

It would be wrong to suppose that no education was possible for women, save such as the nunneries afforded. In his thirty-fourth letter Osbert de Clare writes of a lady who was a governess in Stephen's reign, and who seems to have been treated as one of the family. Home education dates from a very early period. In *Women in English Life*, Miss G. Hill tells us that in mediæval times the demoiselle could often read with fair fluency, while the damoiseau, under the same roof, was unable to sign his name and to spell out the words of his breviary. This would partly arise from a division between the work of man and woman : fighting and the world of sport for him, home and its occupations for her ; and partly from the fact that many manor houses boarded a clerk, or chaplain, who acted as tutor to the young people. Doubtless, in many cases, the girls would be found more docile than the boys. Sir Thomas More, as is well known, taught his daughters to be proficient Greek and Latin scholars.

The honour rendered by the Church to single women was ridiculous in the eyes of Reformers. In the thirteenth century the author of *Holy Maidenhood* had called the nun the free woman ; the wife, the slave. Erasmus styled the nun the slave ; the wife, and indeed all those outside the convent, free. Miss Eckenstein points out how, under Wolsey and Cromwell, the grossest charges against monastic life were, in certain quarters, at once accepted as clearly proved. Sir Thomas More's refutation of these charges, and his

severe criticism of Luther, passed unnoticed at the
time. Even Wolsey received censure from the King
for indecent haste in grasping monastic property. The
stupid falsehood that nunneries were commonly the
refuge of the profligate must be dismissed as baseless.
The Church had herself often held visitations to correct
monastic abuses, usually proceeding, as far as nunneries
were concerned, from inability of the prioress to ad-
minister. The Commissioners who wrote to Cromwell
touching Catesby, could only say they found the house
in perfect order.* The same was true of the White
Ladies at Gracedieu; in Cumberland, rebels restored
the nunnery at Seton; in Yorkshire, the people favoured
nunneries because "our daughters are there brought up
in virtue," as Roger Aske phrased it.

Gasquet, the historian of Henry VIII.'s reign,
declares that "in the convents the female portion of
the population found their only teachers, the rich as
well as the poor; and the destruction of these religious houses by Henry was the absolute extinction
of any systematic education for women during a long
period."

The divine, Fuller, who died in 1661, lived to
recognize that the loss women suffered at the Reformation was heavy. Speaking of the convents, he writes,
"They were good she schools, wherein the girls and
maids of the neighbourhood were taught to read and
work; and sometimes a little Latin was taught them

* See Miss ECKENSTEIN's chapter on the Dissolution in England,
in *Woman under Monasticism.*

therein. Yea, give me leave to say, if such feminine foundations had still continued, provided no vow were obtruded upon them (virginity is least kept where it is most constrained), haply the weaker sex, besides the avoiding modern inconveniences, might be heightened to a higher perfection than hitherto has been attained."

It cannot for a moment be denied that with the Reformation lay the path of progress; and yet women may regret that the Reformers laid such stress upon the theory that there is no career for them outside wifehood and motherhood. Single women have often been in the van in movements affecting their sex; wives and mothers profit by their devotion and enthusiasm. Is it too much to attribute a large part of England's depressed position in the educational world, which has lasted far into the nineteenth century, and from which she is only now emerging, as in some measure due to the failure of Reformers to use and dignify in social work the unmarried woman?

With the theory just stated, grew up that other belittling idea, that education is unnecessary for women; that since they are destined for home life, it would be useless, and even injurious, to cultivate their intelligence. John Lyon, the founder of Harrow Grammar School, in 1571, expressly excludes girls from the benefits of his foundation. They seem to have had only a small share in the many grammar schools founded in the reigns of Henry VIII., Edward VI., and Elizabeth, when the power of the Church of Rome was crippled, and her vast wealth confiscated.

On this point, Richard Mulcaster, master of the Merchant Taylors' School founded in 1561, says: " I set not young maidens to public Grammar Scholes, a thing not used in my countrie, I send them not to the universities, having no president thereof," and goes on to explain that, all the same, young maidens must be taught to read and write, and that these branches, as well as music and languages, have a right to be expected of them. " I dare be bould therefore to admit young maidens to learne, seeing my country gives me leave and her custome standes for me. Their natural towardnesse (aptitude) should make us see them well brought up." (See Miss Hill's chapter on the Scholars of the Sixteenth Century, *Women in English Life.*)

The whole subject of women's education up to recent times is still unexplored territory. It probably varied very much at different epochs and in different families. Though excluded from the grammar schools, and bereft of the education nunneries at one time afforded, it may well have been that girls received in their own homes a very fair education of the kind we now term technical. Those who worked at home had not only to undertake ordinary housework and cooking, but spinning and weaving in early times, and until comparatively recently baked the bread, made jams, pickles, wines, pickled and salted meats, brewed, culled simples, made essences and decoctions, knew a little about surgery and medicine in its easier forms, washed and dressed the linen, made candles as well as all sorts of garments. Most of these occupations are now swept right out of the home ; but as long as they were home duties, women must have found plenty of scope for their activity.

Probably few but the gifted could derive real benefit from the sort of schooling that too often prevailed in grammar schools. It may have been that home education under a clever housewife was more truly educative than much that was labelled education. We know, because the Schools Enquiry Commission of 1865–67 tells us so, that boys in grammar schools sometimes studied Latin five years, and left school unable to read the language. No doubt girls picked up a little English reading and writing at their mother's knee; their spelling was curious, and evidently original.

Women of rank had a better opportunity. We are told of the learning of the Lady Mary, of Elizabeth, and Lady Jane Grey, which, since they were exalted personages, may easily have been exaggerated. But, speaking of women generally, the Renascence failed to touch them. Both the men and women of the time were agreed that learning was not for women. The great Revival only reaches them in the nineteenth century, the natural and necessary complement of the Renascence movement. It grew narrower and narrower without them : first narrowed to one sex, then to a class. We may take the 189 signatures to a memorial presented to the Schools Enquiry Commission in 1867, the majority of which belonged to the educated men of the country, in favour of the "foundation of a place of education for adult female

students," as a definite acknowledgment that education
for one sex had spelt failure—that in future it must
be for all. By a singular coincidence, that very year
the working classes were enfranchised. From that
date onwards the summarized story of women's education is the removal of barriers.

To the seventeenth century, after the failure of
Puritanism to impress itself on the nation as a whole,
we may trace the rise of the idea that women must
be accomplished, render themselves socially attractive,
play, sing, speak foreign tongues, dance; such accomplishments were called "virtues." Even these some
people blamed: Sir Matthew Hale, for instance. They
thought that a woman needed to know nothing save
what pertained to housewifery; to read Sir Philip
Sidney's *Arcadia* was going beyond the bounds.

Protest was often made against the ignorance of
women both by their own sex and by men. Mary
Astell, in 1694, bitterly complains that men denied
education to women. In the eighteenth century, surely
the nadir of women's education, Lady Mary Wortley
Montagu utters the same plaint, bewailing the neglect
of women's minds, and the universal ridicule poured
on a learned woman. "It is criminal," she writes,
"to try to improve a woman's reason," and complains
of the indulgence extended to women's defects, thereby
preventing improvement. Writing to her daughter
about the education of a grand-daughter, she says,
with some bitterness, that "if there was a common-
wealth of rational horses, it would be an established

maxim among them that a mare could not be taught to pace." Earlier in the century no wit but sneered at the educated woman. Swift, Congreve, Smollett, even the much gentler Addison and Steele, had shafts for so outrageous a being. The enlightened Dr. More was alarmed at the capacity of his daughter Hannah, and caused her to discontinue Latin and mathematics. Mrs. Somerville (born 1780) tells us that when she showed signs of rapid advance in mathematics her father, Admiral Fairfax, observed to her mother: "We must put a stop to this, or we shall have Mary in a strait-jacket one of these days."

Still, the numbers of thoughtful and educated women grew. Butts for cheap wit, they performed the invaluable service of accustoming the world to their existence. Foreign writers commented upon the great amount of liberty enjoyed by Englishwomen. "They govern everything despotically in their houses, making themselves feared by the men," writes one. On the other hand, Dr. Ségur, in 1803, sees little difference between the English and the Turkish woman; the former have neither walls nor keepers, yet suffer equal constraint.

Though De Ségur wrote at a later date, such contradictory observations point to a recognised national characteristic, variety in type and standard, to the fact that room is always made in this country for character and capacity, even to the extent of largely disregarding sex distinctions and prejudices.

In what has been written, only the briefest allusion

has been made to the education of men and boys. For a survey to be truly valuable, a comparison would need to be instituted between the sexes.

Generally speaking, the education of women and girls has lagged, and still lags, behind that of the opposite sex. In all probability the difference in the seventeenth, eighteenth, and more especially the early half of the nineteenth century, was greater than now.

Le Blanc observed, that in the last century the sexes did not talk together ; though probably, if he examined the manners, morals, and capacity of the macaroni, dandy, mohawk, he would not entirely blame womankind for the loss of one of the most refined of pleasures.*

To sum up this imperfect survey: The convents were the great "she schools," as the divine Fuller phrased it. The Dissolution found women less prepared for the blow than men. The convent schools disappeared and nothing replaced them. The Reformers, some of them actuated by genuine dislike and dread of monastic vows ; others, profiting by the general grasping at monastic property, and fearing that they might be called on to restore it, preached that there was no career for women save wifehood and motherhood. A marked depression followed in women's position, no satisfactory outlet

---

* See the extraordinary Act passed in 1770 against women seducing and betraying men into matrimony by means of scents, paints, cosmetic washes, artificial teeth, false hair, hoops, stays, &c. By such conduct they were to incur the penalty of witchcraft, and the marriage to be declared null and void.

being found for their talents and energies. During that period they played a less important part in the history of the nation than ever before. Probably they touched the lowest point in 1832, when Lord John Russell's Reform Bill explicitly declared that in all existing Acts concerning enfranchisement, the word person must be taken to mean male person, and the Bill formally disfranchised women. During that time there were always refined and highly-educated women ; but the proportion was very small, and their performances almost invariably excited ridicule. Education was indifferent for both sexes, but especially for women and girls. The inferiority in that period was greater than it is to-day.

PART I.

SECTION I.

Elementary or Primary Education

ELEMENTARY or Primary Education must be taken to mean that which is obtained in the Elementary

Definition. schools of the country, both Board and Voluntary. Such schools receive State aid, in the shape of a Government grant, and must, in return, submit to inspection by officials appointed by the Lords of the Committee of the Privy Council on Education (usually called the Education Department), and accept a body of regulations known as the Code.

Elementary Education does not now simply embrace the three Rs; it includes subjects that some educationists call Secondary—such as Mathematics, French. Yet since education usually terminates at thirteen, or less, in the State schools, little more than the elements can be mastered in such subjects; the bulk of the education given is elementary. A fair number of schools used by the middle classes do not carry education on beyond the elementary stage, and, to be quite correct, should not be styled Secondary. Preparatory schools are not properly elementary, because their curriculum supposes that education will be carried on, perhaps, to the age of eighteen. The great dividing line must at present be marked by State aid and State control, although it will be shown later that some Secondary schools have naturally developed from the Elementary school system.

The recognition of the principle that every child should be educated belongs to the present century, and was clearly formulated by the National Education League, founded at Birmingham in 1869, whose chief object was to secure the education of every child in England and Wales. We find traces of the idea early in the century, in the labours of Bell and Lancaster, and even in the preceding century; but it cannot be said to have grafted itself on the national mind before the present century. The whole story of national education is a working towards the idea of education for all : the tightening of the cord, that none shall escape. We may watch its development in the regulations for children on barges, in travelling caravans, the blind, deaf mutes, and the mentally defective. The development of the idea that education is for each, according to his capacity, is not unconnected in England with the extension of the franchise; step by step they have broadened together.

The mediæval idea was distinctly that education was for those who had good brains, and who wanted it.

In former times Education was for the clever. The right of the poor and clever boy was fully recognized, and, in early times, carefully safeguarded. That these rights fell into such desuetude as to be practically abrogated was not the result of malice, or refusal to cultivate brains wherever they were to be found, but simply the working out of a well-known social law : that everything, unless precautions are taken, tends to work into the hands of the wealthy and well-to-do. Wealth is the mighty centripetal force ; the counteracting centrifugal force would demand education and vigilance on the part of poverty.

The beginnings of education are found in the monasteries. Monks and nuns desired to educate young people who should be their **Monastery Schools.** colleagues and successors. Hence their internal schools. But, in addition, the monasteries were great social institutions with important duties, amongst which was included the teaching of the young. Little is known of these early schools, especially at the time when monasteries were very important, the seventh and eighth centuries. We know that Hilda, of Whitby, summoned Caedmon, the shepherd boy, to the monastery, and there had him taught, with the result that he produced a metrical version of the scriptures in Anglo-Saxon, of priceless value to philologers. Probably something like class division appeared very early, though the cleavage between classes was not so strictly defined as, say, at the beginning of the present century. We read of youths of gentle birth being sent to abbots' houses. The Abbot of Hyde used to educate eight boys, probably heirs to estates, and the Abbot of Glastonbury had some 300 youths pass through his hands at different times. Yet we recognize fully the democratic principle in the Church of Rome. Langland tells us, in his *Vision of Piers Plowman*, how the cobbler's son and beggar's brat turn writer and then bishop. We know that the villein's son could become a priest, because the Constitutions of Clarendon forbad his consecration without his lord's consent.

Later in the Church's history we find not only schools in the monasteries, but connected with cathedrals, in the parishes, and chapter schools,

Cathedral and Parish Schools which were partly managed by the laity. The parish school would seem to be the place where one would naturally expect to find the children of the poor. But probably the difficulties of travelling caused the children of the yeoman and the labourer to learn together, when they learned at all. In cases of exceptional ability—and we must remember that in thinly populated districts it is everybody's business to know all there is to know—the clever child was doubtless known, and probably welcomed.

The Labour Act of 1405 supplies us with a fact amid all this conjecture. It was intended to counteract the scarcity of farm labour, and requires

Education of the Poor. that none is to apprentice son or daughter to a craft in a town, save those whose rent is at least 20*s.*, *i.e.*, a small peasant proprietor, or cotter. It runs on, regardless of grammar, "provided always that every man and woman of what estate or condition that he be shall be free to set their son or daughter to take learning at any manner of school that pleaseth them within the realm."

The Church was then very powerful, though a few years later the Knights of the Shire did propose to confiscate her property for military purposes. The law can only be construed to mean that she declined to have her supplies of clever children cut off.

In the early days the Church was probably able to undertake such education as was wanted; but it is more than probable that her capability ceased com-

A Prayer for efficient Masters. paratively early. In 1179, by a decree of the Lateran Council, the head teacher of every cathedral was directed to assume authority over all other schoolmasters in the diocese; he was to possess the right of granting a licence, without which none was to presume to teach. This marks an important assumption of authority on the part of the Church. The petition of 1447 shows us that she was not fulfilling her heavy task to the satisfaction of all. In that year four clergymen of London presented a petition to Parliament, complaining of the want of grammar schools, of the scarcity of good teachers, and of the large number of uneducated masters who took up the profession of teaching. The clergymen craved permission to found schools and appoint efficient masters in their respective parishes

C

in order to satisfy the great demand for instruction.
The prayer was granted. We know that at this time
the monasteries were decaying, and the towns and
universities making progress. Shortly afterwards a law
was passed making it illegal to send children to
unauthorized teachers. This foreshadowing of the
Teachers' Registration Bill of a later age was aimed
at those who favoured Wycliffe's teaching, and points
to the fact that schools were arising independently of
the Church.

Meantime, it would be very wrong to suppose that
the middle classes or nobility had a passion for education. In a prefatory letter to his *De Fructu*, addressed
to Dean Colet, founder of St. Paul's School, and the
great educational reformer of his day (*d.* 1519), Pace
tells us of the frank opinion of a British parent heard
by him at some tavern feast. " I
Opinion of a
British parent.   swear by God's body I'd rather that
my son should hang than study letters.
The study of letters should be left to rustics."

This idea was modified as time went on, surviving
well into the 18th century, under the form that learning
was not *quite* the thing for gentlemen ; and exists to-day
in some quarters, with a further modification that it is
not the thing for workers.

An idea prevails, indeed some writers (for example,
Mr. G. C. T. Bartley and Dr. J. H. Rigg) state quite
definitely that schools for the people were begun at
the Reformation. We know that some 300 grammar
schools were founded between the reigns of Henry VII.

and James I. ; but it is clear that the share of the poor in these schools was the share of the clever boy. The

Share of the Poor in the Grammar Schools. Schools Inquiry Commission 1865–67 was quite definite on this point: the purpose of the grammar school was to give an education higher than the rudiments, conducted under religious influences, put within the reach of all classes, with special preference for the poor boy apt to learn. The Reformers were too busy about dogma and the division of the spoils to care much about education, excepting Warham, Cranmer, and one or two others. Moreover, the Reformation inaugurated the individualistic era; with all her faults, the Church of Rome upheld a socialist ideal, and the poor boy was safer under her wing than at any time between the Reformation and the uprise of philanthropic aims in the eighteenth century.

It is true that Erasmus had noble ideas on education : it was to be for rich and poor, for girl and boy alike.

Erasmus and More. But More, who shared his ideas, and Erasmus, were not of the Reformation, which the one opposed, and the other gazed on very coldly. They were in the midst of a great movement, and helped in some of its manifestations. They hoped and believed that men would now open their eyes and see, and that a great era was beginning for mankind. So far as England was concerned, More died on the scaffold, and Erasmus only lived to see the great Renascence movement penned up in the channels of the Reformation. Luther emphatically favoured instruction for the whole juvenile population, girls as well as boys, with characteristic energy proving the obligation from the Bible. The acceptance of his view belongs to German rather than English history.

In a speech in the House of Lords in 1869, the Duke of Argyll mildly told his hearers he was "not aware that any English Reformer laid stress upon the subject of national education," and was moreover of opinion that the grammar schools were not meant for the instruction of the people. It is certain that only the middle classes derived much benefit from them.

The Reformation and Education.

If proof is wanted that the Reformation in England was indifferent to popular education, it can be found in the complaint of 1562, when Speaker Williams was in the chair. It was definitely stated in Parliament that a hundred schools were now altogether lacking where, before the Reformation, they had existed.

Schools destroyed and not replaced.

The complaint was general that the poor could get no education: they were being "scrooged out" of the grammar schools, and no provision at all was made for them. So noticeable was this that in 1589 a law was passed which aimed at preventing grammar schools and universities being used solely by the wealthy. It is worth noting that in Scotland the Reformation shewed a very different face to education. This Dr.

Schaible explains by the fact that in Scotland the
Reformation came from below: the
people wanted it, therefore their
needs were considered. In England
they did not want it—they rebelled
to have the old Church and monasteries reinstated:
the Reformation was from above. Not only was there
no improvement in education; it sank to a lower level
than in pre-Reformation times. John Knox proceeded
to promulgate a national scheme of education for
Scotland, wonderfully complete; indeed, in the light
of his limitations it is truly astonishing. The rich
were to be compelled to educate
their own children, and to pay for
the children of the poor. There was
to be a school in every town and populous parish;
thinly populated districts had special arrangements; in
the principal towns there were to be secondary schools;
the universities were to be re-modelled, leaving the
path to them open. Within fifteen years there was
hardly a town or parish in Scotland that had not its
school and schoolmaster.

John Knox's scheme for National Education.

The rich to pay for the poor.

In England the serious lack of schools was greatly
felt and deplored at the close of Elizabeth's reign.
In 1604 the Church obtained the
control of education by means of
certain canons; and during the
century about 700 parish schools
were founded, a number which cannot nearly have
covered the country. Indeed, as Mr. Craik points

The Church obtains control of Education, 1604.

out,* for the next two hundred years the educational
wants of the country were entirely met by private
and voluntary agency.

The end of the sixteenth century saw the beginning
of the great religious struggle between the Church of
England and the Puritans : a struggle that seemed to
end in the defeat of the latter, but which really secured
constitutional freedom for England, and for all those
nations which have turned to her as a model.   One
cannot but wonder whether a longer tenure of power
by the Puritan party than Cromwell's brief rule, would
not have tended to give England more in due season
her national scheme of education.   The Puritans were
the serious party of the Reformation ; they had a grasp
of principles, they were largely the stuff of which John
Knoxes are made, and moreover, a very large proportion
of them were ministers and schoolmasters.   From the
Restoration until Anne's reign closed, omitting that
The Church   of William III., the policy of the
silences Dissent- Government was to silence and
ing Teachers.   harry them out of the land.   In
1709 the Schism Act was passed, forbidding any one
to keep a public or private school unless he were a
member of the Church of England.   The Church was
left in possession ; and about the same time the Society
for Promoting Christian Knowledge began its work.
Practically they found no provision at all for the
education of the poor, and with praiseworthy energy

* In his excellent work, *The State in its relation to Education.*
Macmillan and Co.

they undertook the task. The educational programme was very modest. Children were to be taught in the principles of the Church of England, *i.e.* the catechism,

The S.P.C.K. begins a National system. to read (especially the scriptures), and to write. Modest as it was, the beginning of a national system would appear to be here. The Society began its work in London in 1699 : it opened its first school in 1702. Mr. George C. T. Bartley, in his *Schools for the People*, gives the following figures. It is probable that girls were attending parish schools in the seventeenth century; but Mr. Bartley's are the first definite figures obtainable.

	No. of Schools.		Boys.		Girls.
1704	...	54	...	1386	...	745
1709	...	88	...	2181	...	1221
1714	...	117	...	3077	...	1741

The clergy examined the schools, and indeed scripture was regarded as the great subject. Miss Jourdan states in a pamphlet—*Improvements in Education*—that writing and arithmetic were non-essential for the schoolmistress—her subjects being reading, needlework, and scripture. The reading would seem to have been only necessary for the sake of the scripture, and there was much parrot-like repetition of the Bible, hymns and catechism. To this period belong such extraordinary versions of the catechism as the following :

Samples of Education. "My duty toads God is to bleed in him to fering and to loaf withold your arts withold my mine withold my sold and with my sernth to whirchp and to give thinks

to put my old trast in him to call upon him to
onner his old name and his world and to save
him truly all the days of my lifes end."

———

'My dooty tords my Nabers to love him as
thyself and to do to all men as I wed thou do and
to me to love onner and suke my fazher and
mother to onner and to bay the queen and all that
are pet in a forty under her to smit myself to all
my gooness teaches sportial pastures and marsters
to oughten myself lordly and every to all my
betters to hut nobody by would nor deed to be
trew in jest in all my deelins to beer no malis nor
ated in your arts to kep my ands from pecken and
steel my turn from evil speak and lawing and
slanders not to civet nor desar other mans good
but to lern laber trewly to git my own leaving and
to do my dooty in that state if life and to each it
his please God to call men."

———

"They did promis and voal three things in my
name first that I should pernounce of the devel
and all his walks pumps and valities of this wicked
wold and all the sinful larsts of the flesh."

These extraordinary versions of the catechism were
presented to one of H.M.'s Inspectors, the Rev. W. H.
Brookfield, and appear in his general report on schools
inspected in Kent, Surrey, and Sussex, 1855; they
could equally well belong to the period under consideration.

Miss Jourdan is of opinion that Sunday schools were in existence in England before Mr. Robert Raikes **Sunday Schools.** began the work at Gloucester in 1780, and cites the work of the Rev. Theophilus Lindsey at Catherick in Yorkshire, who on alternate Sunday afternoons taught the children of his parish; though she admits that from the time Mr. Raikes took up the work, it was better organized and developed rapidly. The Sunday schools really taught the children to read, and sometimes to write. In some places the schools assembled three times on Sunday, this being the only day when for some children any education or civilizing influence was possible. It was indeed a period of national glory and degradation. England's empire was growing by leaps and bounds, whilst at the same time the London gin palaces invited the passer-by to get drunk for a penny, or dead drunk, twopence.

Hannah More and her friend Miss Harrison were teaching the poor in back kitchens and barns. They were openly ridiculed, the young women who could have helped standing aloof. These ladies were told **Objections to Education.** that they would ruin agriculture; that if servants learned to read, they would read their mistresses' letters; that if they learned to write, they would forge. Some did not object to religious instruction, as they thought it might prevent the robbing of their orchards. The Sunday school movement grew, the Church of England and Nonconformist bodies alike

developing it. The Ragged School movement dates
a little later.

In the beginning of the century two educational
reformers come to the front, Dr. Andrew Bell and

Bell and Lancaster.

Joseph Lancaster, both claiming to be the inventors of what the *Edinburgh Review* styled that " beautiful
and inestimable discovery," the monitorial system.
Bell was a Scotch episcopalian, and, unlike the generality of his countrymen, fearful of elevating the poor
above their station. Certain persons he regarded as
doomed to the drudgery of daily toil; certain others
were predestined to rank, wealth, privilege. Bell was
cold, shrewd, self-seeking; unable to conceive a national
scheme of education, even if he had had the necessary
qualities to help to carry it out. Nevertheless, he
filled his contemporaries with admiration. R. C.
Dallas, in his *New Conspiracy against the Jesuits*, says
of Dr. Bell's system : " It is impossible to contemplate
the advantages arising to our fellow-creatures and to
society from Dr. Bell's system of education for the
poor, without grateful feelings to the author. . . .
Thousands upon thousands will bless him, while he
yet lives, and a perpetual series of millions will revere
his memory after he shall have joined the myriads
of spirits from whom he shall himself learn the
celestial allelujahs." In 1797 he published a pamphlet
—*An Experiment in Education*—after he left Madras.
He expounds the monitorial system which, briefly
stated, is simply using the older children to teach

the younger.   He had a living at Swanage, and in 1806 caused his method to be introduced to a day school there.   Later, the Archbishop of Canterbury introduced it into a Lambeth school established by him ; the National Society, founded in 1811, took up the work.   Its great feature is distinctive religious teaching. Besides establishing schools, the Society has worked to secure suitable teachers, and at different periods has established five institutions* for the purpose of training them.   Joseph Lancaster (1778–1838) was an educational enthusiast, of a different temperament from Bell. At the age of fourteen he walked to Bristol, with the idea of taking ship to Jamaica, to teach the negroes.   The scheme was prevented by his parents.   Later he became a member of the Society of Friends, and usher in a school.   His skill and zeal brought crowds of children to his school in the Borough Road : to-day, a Board School stands on its site.   Lancaster held that all religious tenets should be excluded from a school meant for the use of all.   Friends came to his aid, the numbers of his scholars outgrew his premises ; even George III. subscribed liberally to extend his work.   As he was very poor, Lancaster also hit upon the plan of using elder scholars to teach the younger ones ; gradually this extended into their being trained as masters.   Lancaster, though most zealous for the advancement of his pupils, was vain, thriftless, and guiltless of business capacity.   When he was arrested

---

* There are other Church Training Colleges, but they are not under the Society's direction.

Rise of the British and Foreign School Society. for debt in 1807, Corston and Fox came forward to found the British and Foreign School Society "with a single eye to the glory of Almighty God, and with a view to benefit the British Empire." The Society spread quickly, paid Lancaster's debts, and extended his system; though later he and they had to part company. The whole movement was for unsectarian religious education; no catechism or peculiar tenets were allowed to be taught. Amongst the objects of the Society were the stimulation of local effort and the training of teachers. The year 1870 saw the adoption in the Education Bill of the principle for which the Society had struggled: undenominational religious instruction. The Society has six training colleges for teachers.

Both Bell and Lancaster deserve praise for the efforts they made to improve popular education. The manufactures of England had recently been revolutionized by the application of steam as a motor power, and by numerous inventions in the arts of spinning, weaving, iron-casting, and so forth. Wealth and population were increasing with incredible rapidity; education, refinement, all those civilizing forces to which we give such comprehensive names as art and culture, were lagging far behind mere industry and the brutality of numbers. Men from whom light and leading might have been expected, bestowed upon material increase such terms as "progress," "advance," "improvement"; as if

"Progress" of the Nation.

these terms referred to the people at large instead of to exports, imports, output, turnover, and the general field of business energy.

To Bell, Lancaster, and to Dr. George Birkbeck, the founder of mechanics' institutes, we are indebted for their practical protest against the idea that mere "progress" is enough for a nation: that the people exist for toil alone.

The Churches had sunk to a low ebb of vigour and vitality; Bell and Lancaster succeeded in enlisting their aid on behalf of education. Their monitorial system has since been condemned; we must judge the value of their work whilst recollecting that the strictest economy was necessary. Very few approved the education of the people, still less were they prepared to spend much of that greatly increasing wealth on so absurd an aim. Of

The National Society.

the two Societies with which they were connected, the National Society, the organized educational agency of the Church of England, was far the larger; but the struggle between the two was partly equalized by the immense vigour and energy of the British and Foreign Society, the Dissenters' agency. It is said that the numerical proportion of the two bodies was as nine to one, and the National Society had the wealth and influence of the Establishment in addition.

The State and Education.

From the end of the eighteenth century it was admitted that the State ought to do something for education, and this duty became even more imperative when

the passing of the First Factory Act in 1802 gave
the children of the workers more leisure. The point
was whether education should be organised from the
centre, or whether the State should cast upon local
authorities the duty of establishing parochial schools,
and using compulsory rates for their maintenance.
Lord Brougham's opinion was that building grants
only would be necessary on the part of the State,
and that each locality should control its educational
machinery.   Much more overwhelming was the religious
difficulty, which instead of lessening, rose steadily, inducing both parties to repeatedly oppose State inter-
Growth of the   vention out of religious jealousy. Lord
Religious   Brougham's important Bill in 1820
Difficulty.   was rejected by the Nonconformists
because, in their opinion, it strengthened the hands of
the Church; the Church defeated Lord Melbourne's
Bill in 1839 because Churchmen considered that it
placed Dissenters almost on an equal footing with themselves; in 1842 the Nonconformists opposed Sir Robert
Peel's Bill.   The most enlightened legislation took for
granted that a teacher must be a member of the Church
of England, and a certificate from the clergyman of the
parish was essential to a teacher's appointment.   Even
in 1840, when the Government had established inspection of schools, it was necessary to concede that the
Primate should sanction the appointment of inspectors.
Nonconformists, suspicious and alarmed, compelled a
power of veto to be granted to the British and Foreign
Society.

While the sects wrangled the children were not taught. Far less than half their numbers were to be found in schools of any kind, and **Inadequacy of the Schools.** these were wretchedly inadequate. In the Abstract of Returns, presented to the House of Commons in 1839, it was shewn that there were parishes in many English counties absolutely without schools. On a single page of the returns there are often as many as four parishes so marked. Of course their population is usually small, but they run up to 300, 400, 500. In one parish, Earsham, there was only one school, attended by 20 boys and 5 girls, though the population was 759.

Instruction, if one may use the word, was often given in a single room used for sitting, sleeping, and cooking. **A Liverpool School.** Complaint is made of the languor of the children, their real inability to do mental work of any kind. Such fetid little dens amply account for it. In Liverpool a school was found in 1840 in a garret, up three pairs of broken stairs. There were forty children in a room ten feet by nine; on a perch in a corner were two hens and a cock, and beneath a stump bed was a dog-kennel with three terriers. The master sat in a position to obscure three-fourths of the light from the one small window. In another Liverpool school no seats were provided, and the children simply squatted on the floor. "In a third school, also in a garret very much dilapidated, and only nine feet by twelve feet, were thirty-eight scholars; not more than six of them had any book; a desk, at which only five boys could be accommodated at the same time, was all the provision for writing and arithmetic. The room below was in the occupation of a cobbler, whose wife lay ill in bed with a fever, himself pursuing his avocation near to the bedside."

"Religious instruction," says the editor of the papers of the Central Society (1837), "is seldom attended to beyond the rehearsal of a catechism, and moral education, real cultivation of the mind, and improvement of character, are totally neglected." "Morals," said one master, in answer to an inquiry whether he taught them, "morals! how am I to teach them to the like of these?" To the same question another master replied, "That question doesn't belong to my school, it belongs to girls' schools." The same authority states that the girls' schools had "a more favourable appearance than the boys' schools; better order and discipline prevailed, and some mistresses appeared to have solid qualifications for their office." Those who collected these facts complained of the conceit and self-sufficiency of the teachers. When the lack of the most necessary equipment was pointed out to them, they retorted that there was no royal road to learning. Much later than this, in 1870, when one of England's twelve largest towns was conducting an enquiry previous to the establishment of some Board Schools, a "school" was found kept by a poor widow in a room 10 feet A "School" in   by 8½. It contained three low
1870.   forms and a few articles of ordi-

nary household furniture; there were no desks, reading books, nor slates. The widow only professed to teach reading, and this with some difficulty, as she had lost the roof of her mouth. Since there were no books, she taught her subject by means of posters on the wall announcing sales by auction, and especially the performances at the local music-hall.

Such educationists and equipment were by no means unique. In the earlier part of the century hardly any means existed for the training of

Unfitness of Teachers.

teachers, and in many cases the mere failures at other trades and crafts took to teaching the young as the last possible resource. It illustrates the ordinary attitude in England towards education, that when it was proposed to displace these ineffectual persons, popular sympathy was largely on their side, since meddlesome people sought to deprive them of their means of earning an honest livelihood. Great complaint was made of the sour temper of the dame schoolmistresses, and its bad effect upon the children. Teachers very largely followed some other occupation. One blind teacher is mentioned who, in the intervals of hearing lessons, turned his wife's mangle. On the occasions when dames had a washing, a neighbour, or neighbour's child, would mind the school.* On being asked the number of her

* See the evidence given before the Select Committee on the Education of the Poorer Classes, 1838. Mr. Gladstone sat on it, and was very wishful the poor children should be taught singing to rouse them out of the languor and lassitude of which everyone complained.

D

scholars, one good lady said she had never counted them, it was unlucky: "Look at the mess David got into by counting the children of Israel." But even whilst education was at this low ebb, it was not

Educational supremacy of Birmingham.
everywhere the same. Manchester does not seem to have been as bad as Liverpool, and it was universally admitted by the witnesses who appeared before the Select Committee of 1838, that Birmingham stood on a different plane altogether. Manchester is said to have had about two-thirds of its children, between five and fifteen, in school for some period of their lives; in Liverpool this was the case with less than half of the children. At the same time, 1833, out of sixty-five schools at Salford, containing 12,000 children, only five were found to be fairly well provided with books. As an illustration of the short period during which children stayed at school, we may take the case of the model school of the British and Foreign School Society, mentioned by Mr. B. F. Duppa in one of the pamphlets issued in 1837 by the Central Society of Education. There were between 500 and 600 children in one room, taught by one master, Mr. Crossley, and monitors. For one year there were 697 entries. Glancing over a large number of figures brought before the Committee, it is evident that the proportion of girls who went to school was very much smaller than that of boys. One example among a hundred is that of the Bethnal Green National Schools, where, in February, 1838, there were 457 boys and 214 girls, and some-

times the girls' schools are marked as closed, or discontinued.

It need hardly be said that illiteracy during this period was rampant. Of 1459 adult paupers in the
Norfolk and Suffolk Unions, in 1838,

Illiteracy in England. 818 could not read or write, and 200 did so very imperfectly. From 1845 to 1850 inclusive, 45 to 49 per cent. of the women who signed the marriage register did so by a X; 31 to 33 per cent. of the men did the same. About 1860 57 per cent. of the British Army were illiterate. The hands of the Government were tied by sectarian bigotry. Churchmen and Dissenters were terrified lest one party should get an advantage over the other.

Nothing can more deserve admiration than the indomitable energy with which private individuals,
societies, and boards, attacked a task

Societies at work. so herculean and apparently hopeless as the education of the people. The State was not ready, but they were. In a few years we find the Home and Colonial Society at work (1836), the Central Society, London Diocesan Board, Congregational Board, Church of England Sunday-school Institute, Ragged School Union, College of Preceptors, Church of England Education Society, besides the Society for Promoting Christian Knowledge, the British and Foreign School Society, and the National Society. These are central institutions, but almost every locality had a society of its own, independent, connected with these or with some of them. In London alone 60 societies arose in 30 years.

Students of English history are well aware that English rights or liberties, charters, and privileges have **How the State** been obtained because Parliament **began to control** retained the command of the purse. **Education.** The Constitution is built upon the sound principle of "no supplies without redress of grievances." It was not because the French and Spanish peoples loved despotism that their States-General and Cortes mildly seconded royal commands; the intensely practical English mind lighted on the means of control, and rarely let it slip. It is characteristic of the national attitude on this question that the State control of Primary Education was inaugurated in 1832 by means of a money grant of £20,000, merely placed in the Estimates without any legislation, and used for educational purposes through the agency of the National Society and the British and Foreign School Society. The summarized history of State control of education in Britain is simply the increase of that sum, and the increase in efficiency of the schools accepting State aid. "Do you want money to help you in your work?" says the Department in effect. "Then you must accept our terms and regulations."

From this first money grant in 1832 originated the creation of the Committee of Council in 1839 to **The Committee** supervise the work. The same **of Council, 1839.** year saw the appointment of the first inspectors, who were to judge if schools deserved the help they claimed, and whose tact and ability have contributed not a little to evolve a system and coherency out of vast numbers of various schools. Two conditions were imposed on all schools receiving the grant. No school was to receive aid unless the Bible were, at least, read in it; there must besides be a conscience clause, permitting parents to withdraw their children from religious instruction. Church schools were exempted from the operation of this clause, being open only to those who accepted her religious teaching.

Mr. Henry Craik points out in *The State in its Relation to Education* how the Government most of all desired to begin a Normal Training College for Teachers, since teachers were the greatest and most pressing need. It was proposed that Nonconformists, availing themselves of such training, should have secular instruction in common with Churchmen, but have religious instruction of their own. The Church bitterly opposed the scheme; it had to be abandoned; and to this day there is no State Training College, the Government simply subsidizing the institutions erected by the sects.

Training of Teachers.

The Government Grant rapidly increased, as shown in these figures:

							£
1832	.	.	.	.	.	.	20,000
1839	.	.	.	.	.	.	30,000
1870	.	.	.	.	.	.	840,000
1882	.	.	.	.	.	.	2,393,000
1894	.	.	.	.	.	.	6,500,000
1896–97	.	.	(estimated expenditure)				7,122,000

The standard of education remained deplorably low. In a careful report on the Midland District in
Lowness of the Standard of Education. 1845 it was found that only about one child in six could read the Scriptures with any ease, and many of these could read no secular book. About one-half the children left school without being able to read; only one in four could write in the most mechanical fashion; not two per cent. could work a small sum in the rule of proportion. This was due to the deplorable ignorance of teachers and to the lamentable monitorial system, which might work well under a zealot like Lancaster, but was an instrument for evil in the hands of the dull and apathetic. Totally ignorant boys and girls were placed in command of classes which could in no way profit by their instruction; the teaching simply meant to keep the children quiet.

An improvement was affected in 1846, when the Government borrowed the pupil teacher system from
The Pupil Teacher System. Holland. Young people were apprenticed to the head-teacher from the thirteenth to the eighteenth year, receiving both payment and instruction for their services. Grants were ultimately given to sectarian training colleges, as already stated, in order to secure better training for intending teachers, largely pupil teachers who had served their apprenticeship and been drafted into the colleges by means of Queen's scholarships. After a two years' course they had to sit for the final examination for the teacher's certificate.

The teacher's parchment is only bestowed after she has successfully taught two years in the schools of the Department. A large but fortunately decreasing proportion of teachers are still not fully certificated, especially in Voluntary Schools. The percentage of untrained are: men, 29·21; women, 50·77. It is of course obvious that to be untrained does not necessarily mean to be incapable.

It is scarcely necessary to dwell upon the operation of Original or Revised Codes, of capitation grants, payment by results, augmentation grants, and other means devised by the Education Department in its attempts to organise national education by gradual rather than sweeping measures. Capable teachers have always grumbled at the cast-iron mould into which the Department has poured them, and doubtless their objections to the system have been well founded. Original and conscientious teachers have certainly suffered; they could have done better with a freer hand. But laws are mostly made for the wicked, and the Department has had to deal with an army of teachers, a large proportion of whom may have meant well, but some of whom were neither capable, efficient, nor well-educated. Payment by results may have harassed the efficient; it has caused the inefficient and the doubtful to keep the pace.

The Revised Code, 1861.

If we survey the field about 1870, we shall find a considerable improvement on the mid-century state of affairs. Accommoda-

Before 1870.

tion had improved, but it was and remains insufficient; there existed no means of bringing the children into the schools; the teachers were not of the same status as they are to-day; pupil teachers were far too largely used, they and a head-teacher often staffing a whole school; the infant schools were little better than nurseries; the standard required of the children was absurdly low. In some manufacturing districts quite young children spent half the day at school and half at the factory. (Half-timers are disappearing. When this paragraph was first written in 1894 they numbered 164,000, chiefly in Lancashire and Yorkshire; in 1896 there were still 127,000 too many.) The main faults of the schools were the dull, soulless monotony, parrot-like repetition, mechanical grinding.

Up to 1870 all that had been done had been achieved by minutes of the Education Department, **Education Act, 1870.** without legislation. In 1870, after a long struggle, embittered by religious prejudice and jealousy, Mr. Forster's famous Education Bill became law, under Mr. Gladstone's First Ministry. The Nonconformists greatly opposed it. Since its passing into law, the Nonconformists have upheld and the Church opposed it. Briefly summarized, the great measure divided the country into school districts, adopting the boundaries of boroughs for towns, of civil parishes for the country. If school accommodation were deficient, or if the **The School Board.** inhabitants desired it, a School Board was to be elected by the ratepayers, empowered to demand from the rating authority the amount required for school provision and maintenance; it was to possess the power of erecting and managing schools. All schools receiving Government aid were to be worked by means of a conscience clause; catechisms and formularies distinctive of particular religious sects were to be excluded from rate-supported schools. School Boards had optional powers to make attendance compulsory between the ages of five and thirteen; they could fix the standard at which a child might leave school, and often they fixed it pretty low.

Genuine educationists were abashed at what the Act left undone; others at what the Government had dared to do. The former noted that education was not compulsory, not free : School Boards failed to cover the country. Yet a great step in advance dates from 1870; all State-aided Church schools had for the first time to submit to a conscience clause. At this time nine schools out of every ten were Church schools. The

Acts of 1876 and 1880. Acts of 1876 and 1880 added to the power of the State arm in education. The former, known as Lord Sandon's Act, set up a new authority, called the School Attendance Committee, for the purpose of enforcing attendance where no School Boards existed. The Act of 1870 did not affect such districts. They were now empowered to form a School Attendance Committee, which, strange to say, was not compelled to make bye-laws com-

Compulsory Attendance. pelling children to attend school. Mr. Mundella's Act in 1880 supplied

the necessary compulsion. The Acts forbad the em
ployment of children below the age of ten. Exemp-
tions from school attendance between the ages of ten
(now eleven) and fourteen are legal if a child has
passed a certain standard, usually the fourth, to be
settled by each Board. Parents neglecting to educate
their children were subjected to penalties; officers,
known as school attendance officers, were appointed
to visit children absenting themselves from school.
The last great link in the chain of State Education

Free Education, 1891. was the Act of 1891, by which education was declared free. Parents
are now authorized to demand free
places in elementary schools for their children. In
1895, 16,493 schools were absolutely free; 3132 continued to charge fees, though admitting free scholars;
only 114 refused what is technically called the fee-grant
of the Department, 10s. per annum for each child, to
replace the payment of fees.

The following statistics of the Education Department, including England and Wales, may be found
useful:

England has, unlike France, a very large child popu-

England's Child Population. lation in comparison with her adult
population. Thus, out of 29,731,000,
the number of children was 7,536,000.
(The figures refer to 1891.) The estimated population
for 1895 was 30,394,000; but probably there is no
alteration in the proportion.

1895. BOYS AND GIRLS.

Number on the school registers receiving elementary education	5,325,000
Present at inspection	4,868,000
In average attendance	4,325,000

GIRLS.

Number receiving elementary education .	(Not known ; no departmental returns).
Present at inspection	2,380,000
In average attendance	2,079,000

Note that ciphers have been substituted for last three figures.

The Education Act of 1891, which came into force in 1892, providing free education wherever parents chose to claim it, has swept a large number of infants between three and five into the schools. The Department inclines to the opinion that it has also increased the attendance of the older scholars. The schools which are not free are chiefly voluntary, and therefore Church schools. In 1895 free scholars numbered 4,519,000, compared with 780,000 paying scholars.

The Department has a great army of teachers working under it :

Number of Teachers.		
	Certificated teachers (*trained* and *untrained*)	53,000
	Assistant	28,000
	Additional	11,600
	Pupil Teachers	30,000
	Studying in Training Colleges and Day Training Departments . .	4,380

Teachers are very variously paid, according to sex, and whether their school is Board or Voluntary :

Payment of   1870. Average pay of Certificated
Teachers.   Head-master .   .   .   £94
              1895   .   .   .   .   . £137

              1870   .   .   .   Mistress £57
              1895   .   .   .   .   .   £87

AVERAGE PAY DISTINGUISHING BOARD FROM
VOLUNTARY TEACHERS.

	Head-master.	Head-mistress.	Mistresses' percentage of Masters' salary.
Church of England . .	£121	... £75	... £62
Wesleyan	£170	... £86	... £50
Roman Catholic . . .	£117	... £66	... £56
British, Undenominational, &c.	£143	... £81	... £56
School Board . . .	£162	... £114	... £70

The pay of teachers is steadily rising; indeed the whole profession stands in a different position from what it occupied in 1870. It is safe to prophesy a further rise in pay, social standing, and popular estimation.

The difference between the pay of masters and mistresses for performing much the same work is

Women paid less than Men. a question specially interesting to women. The authorities at Whitehall have no explanation to offer on the subject. It is worth noting that the percentage of difference between the salaries of a Board schoolmaster and mistress is less than in the Voluntary school.

An increasing proportion of women teachers are being employed in the elementary schools of the

Proportion of Women Teachers. country. In 1869, for every 100 teachers of each class, 48 certificated, 60 assistant teachers, and 57 pupil teachers were women and girls. In 1894 the proportions had increased to 60 certificated teachers, 82 assistant teachers, and 79 pupil teachers. The teachers in the Infants' Department are all women. (For the figures see page 166).

How the cost of Elementary Education is met. The cost of Elementary Education in England and Wales is met in two principal ways :

(*a*) A grant from the Imperial Treasury, estimated to be, for 1896–97, £7,122,000. The Education Department distributes this sum to School Boards and Boards of Managers of Voluntary schools. The efficiency of a school, as judged by the report of the inspector, or result of an examination, the adequacy of the staff, the state of the buildings, the previous record, are all taken into consideration in allocating the grant.

(*b*) Local moneys raised thus :—(1) Local rates paid to the local School Board by the rating authority. Board schools are the only rate-supported schools. The rates collected for this purpose in 1895 amounted to £1,942,000. (2) Voluntary contributions, usually raised through religious agencies for the support of Denominational schools which receive no aid from the rates. The chief of these are the Church of England and Roman Catholic schools. The sum raised in 1895 in voluntary contributions was £836,000, of which less than £2,000 was devoted to Board schools. Voluntary contributions show a tendency to fall off, though they have slightly risen for the last year or two.

The cost per child in Voluntary schools in 1895 was £1 18s. 11¼d.; in Board schools, £2 10s. 1¾d. The first sum is chiefly made up by grant

The Cost per Child. (from all sources), voluntary contributions, endowment, school-pence. The second by grant (from all sources), rates, school-pence. The earning of Government grant is commonly regarded as a test of efficiency: Voluntary schools earn 18s. 5¼d. per head; Board, 19s. 5d.

The numbers of children in Voluntary schools are 2,445,000; in Board, 1,879,000. The latter have shewn a tendency to gain upon the former,

Numbers of the Children. and, in the main, possess better buildings and equipments, more highly certificated and better paid teachers, the result of having more funds at their disposal.* It is only fair to state that many village schools are Voluntary, having always been under the wing of the Church of England. Many Churchmen claim that such schools need aid from the rates; those who are opposed to sectarian education sometimes admit this claim, but advance a counter claim for control by the ratepayers.

* Sir John Gorst freely admits the inferiority of the Voluntary schools. Comparing them with the Board schools, he states: "They have worse buildings, worse apparatus, worse paid teachers, assistants with inferior qualifications, and larger classes for these teachers to instruct." (See his article in the November number of the *Nineteenth Century*, 1896.)

The standard of education in the Elementary schools cannot be termed high, though of recent years a marked

A Typical Elementary Curriculum. improvement has been visible. The following is a typical curriculum in a girls' school : — reading, writing, arithmetic, two class subjects (English, geography, history, sewing, singing) ; one specific subject (algebra, chemistry, domestic economy, French, cookery). Drill is now commonly taught to both sexes; without it, the higher grant cannot be earned.

The difference in the curriculum for boys and girls is that drawing is compulsory for boys, sewing for girls.

How Girls specialize too early. A Treasury rule lays down that a girls' school cannot earn the drawing grant unless cookery is taken ; and practically this is prohibition. In order to proceed further in sewing, the teacher may also take it as a class subject instead of history or geography ; inspectors are instructed to accept a lower standard of arithmetic from girls than from boys, because of the encroachment on their time by cooking and sewing. In many cases four or five hours weekly are spent upon sewing. Thus girls lose the cultivation of their powers of observation by drawing ; neglect history and geography, by which the mental horizon is widened ; have the training in precision and accuracy, which arithmetic can give, relaxed. All this to gain skill in a handicraft for which they have seldom shewn much liking,* and which is

---

* The keeping of girls to the needle was a great business in olden times. The elder ladies seem to have found that it depressed

largely rendered useless by the sewing machine, and by the growing custom among all classes of buying ready-made garments, especially woven garments, which are rapidly superseding all others. Those who are not convinced that there is a great expenditure of time upon so uneducational a subject as sewing, should attend the admirable exhibition of the work of children under the London School Board, in the Hugh Myddelton Schools, Clerkenwell, held annually in July. The most elaborate garments, such as small dresses, petticoats and pinafores with lace insertion, were ticketed, in 1896, as having been worked by children of six or seven, with hardly any assistance from the teachers. On the other hand, the importance of drawing can scarcely be over-estimated. "The chief object of the craftsman," observes one of H.M. Inspectors, "as of everyone else engaged in education, is the training of the eye. . . . It is the schoolmaster's duty to train faculties, and not to develop facilities ; it is waste of time to teach at school what can be as well or better taught in the business of life."

It has been laid down as a rule by the authorities on Technical Education, that no trade or employment **Early specializa-** shall be directly taught in elementary **tion bad for boys.** schools. Thus, if a boy means to be a carpenter, he cannot learn carpentry as part of the school curriculum until he has passed Standard IV.

the spirits of the younger ones, making them more amenable to control. Consequently the needle was greatly praised.

It is remarkable how sound educational axioms seem to be flung to the winds in the case of girls ;* for them, sewing begins in the infant school. School Boards and Education Departments alike seem to conspire to deprive girls of that broader general training which is necessary even to technical skill. And now we see small children of eleven learning cookery, housewifery, laundry work, as if little girls could not be too early pressed into a narrow mould. Authorities on the employment of women can shew that inability to draw even moderately well, the lack of preciseness which arithmetic is supposed to inculcate, is injurious to them when they enter the labour market, as they do by millions. Of course there could be no objection to spending an hour a week upon sewing, since the hand requires to be trained ; nor to older girls learning cookery, laundry work, and so forth, in Technical or Evening Continuation schools, at the age of 16, or thereabouts. Some authorities hold that no difference should be made between the education of the sexes before the twelfth year ; if sewing is good for girls up to that age, for the same reasons it would be good for boys.

A grievance of women until quite recently was that no woman filled the post of inspector, except a directress of needlework. In the spring of 1896 **Women as Inspectors.** the Education Department appointed two qualified ladies as sub-inspectors,

* See Mrs. STANTON BLATCH on this subject in the *Journal of Education*, Oct. 1894.

E

and, moreover, placed them on the same footing as men with regard to pay and other conditions. These appointments gave great satisfaction. It is worth noting that India has had women as inspectors of schools ever since 1880.

It is evident from what has been written that the present century has seen momentous changes in the **Weak points in** educational world. Much has been **the Elementary** done, and much more remains to do. **System.** Speaking generally, the teaching in the infant department and upper standards is relatively better than in the lower standards, from the second to the fourth inclusive. It is noteworthy that the numbers are very large in these, especially as compared with the upper standards. The following are weak points in the English Elementary System:

(i.) The attendance in elementary schools is poor. Not only are some districts backward in enforcing **Attendance.** attendance, but the children attend irregularly when on the registers. The average attendance for every 100 is 81·61. Allowance must be made for the fact that very young children, from 3 years of age, now go to school and bring down the percentage by irregular attendance. But even the older children's attendance is 86·91. England is far behind Germany in regular attendance; the most trumpery excuse is too often urged and accepted for absence from school.

(ii.) The size of the classes is sometimes enormous; 70, 80, 90, and even 100 have been found in one class.

Size of Classes. This of course almost prohibits personal relationship between teacher and pupils, it lessens and even nullifies the teacher's great weapon of influence. The Department recognizes the importance of smaller classes, and is taking measures to secure them.

(iii.) Children are permitted to leave the schools at a very early age. Provided she has passed the sixth **Leaving too young.** standard at eleven, a child may leave at that age, wholly exempt from school attendance. The time has surely now come when no child shall be permitted to leave before the age of fourteen. The half-time system needs to be abolished. The child who has passed the third standard in the country, the fourth in a town, may usually become a half-timer.

(iv.) Pupil teachers are far too much left in control **Pupil Teachers.** of classes numbering 30 children, and sometimes more.

These are the chief defects of the internal regulation of the schools. External influences hamper them not a **Bad External Conditions.** little, notably the bad conditions of life in certain quarters of London and other great cities. Exorbitant rent acts almost as a prohibitive of personal cleanliness and decency. Many children are ill fed and ill clad, ill kept, and even dirty. The Board schools in large cities, especially London, have a large proportion of such children to deal with. Few schools fail to attach importance to manners and personal cleanliness; but bad social conditions make the teacher's task one of grave difficulty.

One might have imagined that in a country where the extremes of wealth and poverty strike the intelligent visitor more than any other feature of our social system, all classes alike would have combined to secure the easy development of the elementary schools, their increased efficiency and attractiveness. Speaking generally, the schools are popular and appreciated, the children are bright and happy.* Yet a section of the nation, largely though by no means entirely the wealthy and comfortable, from the Prime Minister downwards, persistently oppose the levelling up of

Education begrudged.

the schools, especially the Board schools, and every now and then make bitter attacks upon them, proposing to cut down the expenditure. Notably is this the case with the London School Board, which has on the whole performed satisfactorily a task of unparalleled magnitude and difficulty. It pays its teachers well, and as a result has men and women of character and capacity—many of them the real missionaries of London—in its service. Within ten years the London School Board has received 109 complaints from Vestries, District Boards of Works, and other bodies. Numerous other complaints and

* Dr. Buddensieg, Principal of the Government Training College at Dresden, visited three London Board schools in September, 1896. He observed afterwards how much he was struck by the happy and interested expression of the children.

votes of censure on the growing expenditure of the Board have been prepared, but failed of acceptance by the majority. Such facts are an instructive comment upon the much lauded English public spirit. The School Boards, in particular, have to deal with the lower and poorer classes, and even those on the borderland of vice. The mere diminishing the numbers in the classes, a highly necessary reform, will add to the expenditure of the schools ; and those who realize its importance, hope for it at the earliest possible date. The greater wealth of the Board schools has undoubtedly led to the levelling up of the Voluntary schools : they have led the movement.

Mention must be made of the higher grade or upper standard schools, in which education is continued

Higher Grade Schools. to the age of about sixteen. It is stated that the education of girls is more commonly carried on to such an age than that of boys, who go to work earlier. Lower standards are of course also part of such schools, the work of the upper standards being additional to the rest, and apt to result from the energy of capable teachers and Boards which avoid the cheese-paring policy.

School Boards have also devised what is known as Pupil Teachers' Centres. In the past, head teachers

Pupil Teachers' Centres. trained the pupil teachers before and after regular school hours ; a plan both wasteful and unsatisfactory. Pupil teachers are now grouped at centres, of which the

London School Board alone has twelve, where 2400 students of both sexes are taught together. An arrangement is made by which the time of the pupil teacher is divided between the school to which she is attached and the centre, and, so far, the results have been excellent. Many Boards permit Voluntary pupil teachers to avail themselves of the privileges of instruction at the centre upon easy conditions. Similar arrangements are made with regard to instruction for children at cookery, laundry, and housewifery centres. As time goes on, the Kindergarten system is adopted more and more for young children. At three years of age the Education Department recognizes the youthful scholar; she begins the onerous work of earning a grant for the school. A few are sent below this age, so that it is necessary to adopt Kindergarten methods in teaching children of such tender age. The infant schools up to 1870 were mere nurseries; but in the best of the Kindergartens attention is paid to Froebel's principles, now gaining ground more and more. In the great three-block schools it is common to find nearly three-sevenths of the total number of children in the infant school. In the upper divisions reading and writing are usually well advanced when the child is ready for Standard I.

The early age at which English children may leave school has led to a further development of the Elementary system by means of **Evening Continuation Schools.** Evening Continuation schools, which were organized under the Code of

1892. At first they were indifferently attended, and hasty persons styled them failures, at least as far as London was concerned. The judgment was premature, for in 1895 these schools were attended by 270,000 scholars, the majority of whom pay for their instruction. The list of subjects is lengthy, and though the three Rs are still the most widely taught, the report of the Committee of Council states that the curriculum will probably be technical in character. The schools largely replace the night schools of former days, and are partly taught by day-school teachers. There is great need for them in country districts, where educational opportunities are few. Unhappily scholars also are few, so that there is a need for voluntary teachers, who, it is said, were more easy to find when the old night schools were at work than nowadays.

The Education Department has gradually extended its authority over eighty schools for blind and deaf **The Blind, Deaf-** children. 1460 are in schools for **mutes, and Men-** the blind; the deaf number almost **tally defective.** 3000. Besides these, there are schools for mentally defective children, not yet paid for on a higher scale than the ordinary elementary school. The London Board maintains 26 such centres for special instruction, under Mrs. Burgwin's superintendence; there are about 900 afflicted children in average attendance.

Strange to say the Department has not yet oversight of the Poor Law schools, in which pauper children are boarded and educated. These schools are under the supervision of the Local Government Board. Complaint was at one time rife as **Poor Law Schools.** to the indifferent treatment these children received, and the large number who turned out social failures. To-day better theories and conditions prevail. The children are not to blame for the misfortunes, folly, or even wickedness, of their parents; in any case, the aim must be to produce the best possible citizen out of the material. This is now clearly recognized, and has worked a revolution in the environment of the children. The best testimony to the value of better treatment is their improved appearance, health, and the positions they take on leaving the schools. A difference of opinion exists as to the value of the "barrack school," *i.e.* children massed together by hundreds, or the "cottage home" system, where they live together a score in one building. At the first blush, the latter seems to have more in its favour. But there are two objections to be urged against it. The first is the loss of influence by separation from them when the master and matron are both thoroughly capable and kind. The second is the difficulty of finding entirely suitable persons for the cottages, which, with twenty children in them, can never bear a strong resemblance to either cottages or homes.

Elementary Education in Wales. The history of Elementary Education in the Principality of Wales is not devoid of interest. Wales is a poor country; except at Cardiff and Swansea, its interests are mainly bound up in mining, fishing, and agriculture. Until the Government began to pay grants in aid, education was chiefly conspicuous by its absence. And at first the grants were looked upon with distrust, for the Welsh are emphatic in their dissent from the Episcopalian Church; it has been said that some thought grants must be a device to gain their adhesion to it.

The British and Foreign and National Societies were never very active in Wales; and for this reason, as well as the poverty of the country, education in the mid-century is said to have been at an even lower ebb than in England.

The Committee of Council in 1846 directed that an inquiry should be made into the state of Welsh

The Inquiry of 1846.
Education, especially into the means afforded the labouring classes of acquiring a knowledge of the English language. As the Commissioners did not know Welsh, they used interpreters; they drew up what reads like a very frank account of what they saw and heard, so much so that they evoked an outburst of fury on the part of the Welsh.* Mention is made by one Commissioner of the "widespread disregard of temperance, . . . of chastity, of veracity, and fair dealing" in Wales; a second alludes to "drunkenness, blasphemy, indecency, sexual vices, and lawlessness"; a third tells us of social and moral depravity. Many large districts had no schools

---

* See the account of Welsh Education in Messrs. Swan Sonnen-schein's *Cyclopædia*.

at all; seventy-two parishes in Brecknock, Cardigan, and Radnor were so situated.

The schoolroom, where it existed, was the teacher's living room, the loft over a chapel stables, or churches and chapels themselves. A roof or floor without holes, a fireplace, a window capable of admitting sufficient light or any air were uncommon. A few trained and able teachers were to be found; but many of them carried on their teaching with such honest callings as broom and clog-making, cow-keeping, etc. The teacher might be porter, barber, sexton, publican, matron to a lying-in hospital, drover; and some received parish relief. Not a few were devoid of the rudiments of education; and so ignorant of English, the language in which they professed to teach, that the Commissioners could only speak to them through interpreters. School registers were unknown; even the model school at Newport had none. State aid began a better era, the Welsh people being truly appreciative of education. After the Revised Code of 1861, 600 schools were found in the country. H.M. Inspector reported that "the prospects of education were sufficiently hopeful and encouraging."

Poverty of the Welsh Schools.

After the Act of 1870, School Boards multiplied rapidly, because Church schools are displeasing to the majority of the people. Welsh School Boards now number 328, as against 2159 in England, the former being relatively more numerous. From 1870 onwards Welsh educational development has been more assimilated to

Welsh School Board.

that of England. Special instructions are issued by
the Education Department that Welsh may be used
side by side with English in the schools of Welsh-
speaking districts, in order to facilitate intelligent
comprehension. Inspectors make use of Welsh to
test the children. It is perhaps worth noting that
the Welsh earn a proportionately larger grant than
the English schools. Omitting the capital charges in
1894–95—

	England spent		Wales spent
Rates	56·7	...	49·4
Grants, fees, &c. . . .	43·3	...	50·6

(N.B.—Only Board schools may use the rates.)

Education is cheaper in Wales than in England :
Each Board school child cost the State and municipality
in 1895 £2 4s. 4½d., whereas in England the cost
was £2 10s. 7½d. The total number of elementary
schools in Wales is 1467, of which 725 are Board
schools.

In closing this brief survey of the Elementary Education of England and Wales, it may perhaps be well
to call express attention to the great
Great changes in Elementary Education. changes which have taken place. It
is not uncommon to hear fairly
intelligent secondary teachers allude
to the work of the Education Department as if the
Revised Code of 1861 and the system of payment
by results were still in full force. This would appear
to shew the isolation in which teachers—especially, it is
to be feared, women-teachers—are often content to work.

Payment by results has almost disappeared. It first took the form of payment on individual passes; then a percentage of passes, modified by means of a merit grant, so that the conscientious and intelligent teacher might not be too hard pressed. When payment for individual passes was abolished, the Government grant still depended upon the annual examination; Her Majesty's Inspector examined classes chosen by him from the standards, to which the teacher had the right of adding a certain number. Under the Code of 1896 the grant was made to depend, in all but a few cases, upon two or more annual surprise visits by Her Majesty's Inspector. This important change

Grant now depends on inspection.

was largely due to representations made by the National Union of Teachers, a powerful professional organization. Elsewhere it has been pointed out that the success of this revolution depends upon the thorough conscientiousness of the teachers. The following concise *résumé* may show more clearly the steps by which the Department has reached its present method of allocating the grant:

1. Individual passes + fixed grant.

2. Percentage of passes + merit grant + fixed grant.

3. Variable grants in accordance with general efficiency, tested by the annual visit of H. M. Inspector with notice.

4. Same as No. 3, but tested by two or more annual visits without notice.

The Department thus scarcely deserves the oft-urged accusation of rigidity, if we look at its operations over a sufficiently lengthy period. The curriculum has been greatly expanded; the Code is so often altered, that the N.U.T. issues yearly an edition of 20,000 copies, annotated and simplified, so that its members may readily comprehend the frequent changes. The inward meaning of the changes simply testifies to the fact that the Department can now trust the teachers, as it was unable to do in the earlier years of its existence.

A recent addition to the staff of the Education Department testifies to its readiness to ascertain what is being done in the world of education, and its desire to profit by the experience of other nations. In 1895, during the Vice-Presidency of the Right Hon. A. H. D. Acland, the section known as Special Inquiries and Reports was instituted, the directorship of which was accepted by Mr. M. E. Sadler. The Report of the Committee of the Council on Education, 1894–95, states that "the increasing importance and complexity of the questions which are now constantly arising for our decision have rendered it necessary for us to have the assistance of an officer charged with the special duty of keeping, so far as may be found practicable or expedient, a systematic record of educational work and experiments, both in this country and abroad." The Director also supplies the Department with information upon any special question connected with educational matters, and to this end sometimes spends weeks, or it may be months, abroad. Part of the educational library of the S. Kensington Museum, viz., books on pedagogy and educational administration, have recently been removed to 43, Parliament Street, the close neighbourhood of the offices of the Education Department, where it will be more useful for purposes of reference than in its late location. The library will be opened to the public at convenient hours, and is to be placed under the charge of the Director of Special Inquiries and Reports. Both these and other changes testify to the increasing scope and activity of the Education Department.

It may here be noted that there is less differentiation in the elementary education of the sexes than in any other section. The exceptions, the too early specialization of girls in sewing and its results, as well as the tendency for girls to stay later at school than do boys, have been commented on in their place.

VISIT TO A BOARD AND A VOLUNTARY SCHOOL

It was suggested to the writer that it might be well to visit typical Board and Voluntary schools, and to record the most noteworthy features visible on a brief visit. The two schools were recommended by a competent judge as excellent of their kind, and were not selected by the writer. Both lie within the four-mile radius of St. Paul's, and a whole morning was devoted to each.

The Voluntary school was the first visited. It forms one of the usual three-block type: girls, boys, infants; each department separate under its own head. The girls' school is in good buildings, rather picturesque to view, but not properly adapted for the purpose, since they are used for a Sunday school and, probably, for parish or Church meetings likewise. They consist of one large main hall, one large and one fair-sized class-room. Since the classes number five, this means that three classes must be held in the large hall. These the mistress had carefully partitioned from each other by means of curtains; but curtains have a way of gaping, and the noise made by each class was more than audible to the other. Moreover, the small class-room was reached through this hall, an additional disadvantage.

The mistress had held her certificate prior to the days of Board schools; she appeared a woman of wide experience, kindly, capable, ready to move with the times, to profit by the changes now taking place. It was evident that, given these buildings and conditions, the best possible was being done for the children.

An evident disadvantage was the small playground; of this, the boys had half, the remaining half being for girls and infants. Girls and boys would each number about 350; infants, 400. Of course, girls and infants use the playground at different times. Another disadvantage was the under-staffing of the school, a result of its poverty. Two assistants, on leaving, had their classes and salaries divided among the remaining five teachers. The classes are no larger than Board schools often have, the largest appearing to be 70 on the books, which usually means 60 present. Excellent lessons were being given in geography, arithmetic, and so forth; one class of a dozen little girls, backward in arithmetic, was being taught by a senior scholar, who had concrete examples of tens and hundreds in small bundles of sticks. In another class, the girls were being measured in inches for their height, each total being reduced to feet. On inquiry, the salaries of the teachers were ascertained to be : head-mistress, £150 and a house ; the five assistants earn from £50 to £90, only the last being a trained mistress. Four assistant teachers are therefore ex-pupil teachers, without even the moderate equipment that a Training College course affords. The mistress of the infants has £110 and a house. She has five ex-pupil teacher assistants, with salaries varying from £45 up to £70. The infant mistress herself has to give lessons to her pupil teachers between 8.30 and 9.30 a.m.; a pleasant preparation for dealing with large classes of small children in the heat of July.

Talking to the head-mistress of the girls' department over the difficulty of retaining her capable teachers, she observed that, although personally they were loyal to herself, they were constantly drafted into Board schools, where better pay and conditions obtain, leaving with many regrets.

Amongst the advantages of this school the mistress named the supervision and kindly help and advice of the vicar under whom she worked. The children here pay 3d. weekly as school-pence, and this fact, as well as a rather superior neighbourhood, tends to bring better-class children to the school. They are particularly neat, clean, and well-mannered. The mistress explained that a widow's children are taken free, and the pence are also remitted when the bread-winner is out of work. Although the school furniture is not up to date—far too big girls sitting at small desks—yet the rooms are clean, bright, nicely ornamented with flowers. Another advantage in dealing with better-class children is that they can do a little home-work—not much more than a quarter of an hour, but enough to prove that they can take a few steps alone. Some of the girls of the first class—a composite class made up of sixth, seventh, and ex-standard girls—attend cookery and laundry classes at the nearest centre; domestic hygiene is taught in the school itself.

The Board school visited is in a neighbourhood not nearly equal to that of the Voluntary school. It is a free school, and the class of children poorer and not well kept. The girls' dress contrasted disadvantageously with that of the boys in the same school: the boys' close-cropped hair and closely fitting garments must be more convenient in one or two-roomed tenements than a mop of unkempt hair; the girls' washable dresses and pina-fores did not manifest any recent acquaintance with the wash-tub. Every class has its separate room, both for boys and girls; every one of these was entered. They are well kept; the extremely plain walls, of rough brick, painted or coloured, are hung with school pictures and illustrations. Much is said against Board school manners, but, doubtless, coarse, careless parents must bear almost all the blame. In every class the children rose as the visitor entered or left the room, the master observing that outside he could hardly expect them to behave differently from the ordinary gamins. Both the master and mistress are suitable people for the work they have undertaken, entering it much in the spirit of missionaries, and with considerable zeal.

Salaries are higher than in Voluntary schools. The income of the head-mistress is £192, rising £4 yearly (no house); that of her assistants, £85 to £125, the latter being a maximum. Each of these is a trained teacher, equal to the head in all but experience. The latter was asked if the London School Board objects to untrained mistresses: "I am not sure; but I do," was the emphatic reply. The size of the classes is much the same as in the Voluntary school, about 60; the mistress readily admitted that in such classes there can be hardly any study of individuality in mind or character. The young scholar must be drilled into a certain groove, and out of it can hardly step. No homework can be attempted at this school, home conditions not permitting of it. The mistress stated, as a result of previous inquiry, that most of her girls go to bed at 10, 11, and even midnight, just when their parents do, since ordinarily the living room is used at night as a bedroom. Boys play in the basement of the school, girls on the roof, and, strange to say, the girls have the largest playground. However, atonement is made by the boys using it for drill purposes. The Board school girls were found to be very young: whereas in the Voluntary school, in the upper class, a fair sprinkling of the girls were fifteen or sixteen, the Board girls of Standard VI. had only a few as old as thirteen, most being twelve. The great thing in certain districts is to join the ranks of wage-earners at the earliest possible time. In the Board school is a lending library of suitable books, a small museum, and in several class-rooms were such natural history illustrations as tadpoles developing into frogs. The boys' school has only one pupil teacher, the girls' two. One of these was busy teaching foreign children, of whom the neighbourhood has a large number, to read English, many of them coming to school scarcely knowing a word.

Just as the Voluntary school can be greatly benefited by the constant interest of a vicar, who is also an educationist, so the London Board school has outside visitors, called managers, one of whom entered the mistress's room on the occasion of the writer's visit Of the three managers, one takes oversight of the drains and lavatories, one has charge of a country holiday fund, the third accompanies scholars to galleries and museums. Through the kindness of some outsider, a nurse occasionally visits this school, attending to cuts, bruises, sore eyes, deafness, and such like ailments. Much is said touching the extravagance of the London School Board. The mistress stated that on the school premises are some capital spray baths, out of repair, and which the Board declines to put in order for the use of the girls. It seems a pity that where baths are so greatly needed, and where home circumstances make personal cleanliness almost impossible, the intolerable strain of dirt could not be relieved.

Both the Voluntary and Board school mistresses are relieved of responsibility for any special class, and use their time in supervision and the teaching of special subjects in the different classes. Both are Church-women, and greatly impressed with the importance of religious instruction. In the Church school, every day a Scripture lesson, either Bible or Catechism, is given, lasting 40 minutes ; in the Board school the Bible lesson lasts 30 minutes. It is hardly necessary to refute the careless statement that there is no religious teaching in Board schools. In the boys' rooms, there was hanging a carefully arranged Scripture time table, covering several months. Both mistresses and master were emphatic in their declaration that no religious difficulty exists in the schools. The Voluntary mistress has had a few scholars withdrawn from the Catechism lesson ; the Board mistress has Roman Catholics and young Jewesses withdrawn from her Scripture instruc-tion. The latter had been mistress of a Voluntary school in Leicester, commonly supposed to be a freethinking community ; but even there no practical difficulty had ever arisen.

Both ladies commented on the readiness of the Education Department to alter codes and regulations, to make room for the teacher's individuality, to consult the needs of a neighbourhood. They found excellent advice and help in the inspectors, from whom they had received valuable suggestions. History and geography were scarcely taught in one of the schools, an occasional reading lesson or so summed up the instruction in these subjects ; they were very little taught in the other. The time of the girls is encroached upon by domestic economy, and especially by sewing and knitting. In one school, the time devoted to sewing and knitting is four and a half hours weekly. Neither lady seemed to recognize the danger incurred and loss suffered by too early specialization : and it is probable that such recognition will not proceed from women. The Board school teacher stated that the majority of women teachers working under the London Board are Church-women.

SECTION II.

Secondary Education

SPEAKING broadly, Secondary Education embraces all that lies between Elementary Education and the universities or colleges of university rank. As has been already shown, Elementary Education is distinctly on the up-grade. It is both widening and deepening; the better class of elementary schools have already taken, or are preparing to take the position of what the Schools Inquiry Commission of 1865–67 called the Third Grade of Secondary Education. Especially is this the case with the Higher Grade schools, many of which must be regarded as doing secondary work. These schools supply a real need; and as they obtain grants from the Education Department on the ordinary conditions set forth in the Code, it is easy to see that a hard and fast line between Elementary and Secondary Education is not possible. Such Higher Grade schools are not confined to Board schools, but may be found also working as Voluntary schools.

Definition.

It may perhaps illustrate the confusion and even chaos that exists in Secondary Education, and especially on the border-line dividing it from Elementary Education, if two quotations are made from speakers at the Oxford Conference on Secondary Education,* held

Chaos of English Secondary Education.

* *Report of a Conference on Secondary Education.*

70

in 1893. Alluding to the Higher Grade schools, Dr. (now Sir Joshua) Fitch said "They are not Secondary schools"; the Secretary of the Association of Head-masters of Higher Grade and Organized Science schools, describing his own school as typical of the rest, declared "It is not at any rate anything like a Secondary school." The wisdom of the Royal Commission of 1894–95 decided otherwise: "The Higher Grade Elementary schools are really secondary in their character." Such conflicting statements by the authorities illustrate the difficulty of classification. At this Conference the Rev. E. F. M. MacCarthy, Head-master of one of King Edward VI.'s Schools at Birmingham, stated that "Despite the reforming operations of the Charity Commissioners, the chaos of Secondary Education has increased since 1867, owing to the effect of the Education Act of 1870, and the subsidies granted for the purposes of Technical Education."

The share that was given to girls in the old endowed **Share of Girls in the Grammar Schools.** grammar schools, which provided the Secondary Education of the country for a lengthy period, is problematical. Miss Emily Davies tried to convince the Royal Commissioners of 1865–67 that where girls were not expressly excluded from the endowment, as at Harrow, they were included; but though favourable to the education of girls, the Commissioners could not agree with her. We have already seen how Richard Mulcaster, favourable to girls' education, and deeply impressed with their abilities and achievements, writes in

1581 that it is "not the custome of my countrie to set young maidens to public grammar scholes," though by this expression he may simply have meant his part of the country. A writer in the *Quarterly Review*, vol. 146, says it is evident that boys and girls were put on a level in the old grammar schools, since quaint little figures of each still stand over venerable portals in old market places. He quotes Crewkerne, in Somerset, where, he says, the boys simply took possession of what was meant for both sexes.

In the well-known case of Christ's Hospital we stand on certain ground. The famous hospital was certainly

Girls at Christ's Hospital. meant for the poor and for both sexes ; for many years it was largely used as a foundlings' home. Bishop Ridley speaks of the "thousands of poore silly (weak) members of Christ, who were holpen and brought up in it." In the great hall to-day hangs Verrio's picture shewing fifteen girls and as many boys, kneeling, received at an audience granted by James II. But the hospital was governed by men, and, moreover, by wealthy men. The Schools Inquiry Commission of 1865–67 found the usual results of such government: 1124 boys, chiefly of the well-to-do classes, were then being educated in it, and 22 girls. Undoubtedly in the case of a foundling hospital there existed no reason whatever for special advantages for boys. The whole question as to the share of girls in the grammar schools is of interest, and more than a mere archæological interest. England has always carefully avoided a uniform policy, and it may well have been that in certain towns and districts where girls' education had flourished under the wing of the monastery, provision was made for its continuance, even though these cases may have been a small minority. A very general result of the Reformation was that girls were shut out of the secondary schools, and that during the seventeenth and eighteenth centuries they betook themselves to the cultivation of the noxious brood of "accomplishments." Knowledge for itself was an insufficient aim; it might be sought for what it would bring. The boarding-school system grew up, especially during the eighteenth century, as the great forcing-houses of accomplishments, where education was "finished" in the most complete sense of the term. Mrs. Makins' prospectus shows us what was regarded as a good educational programme at that time. This excellent lady opened a "ladies' school" in 1693, near Tottenham High Cross, "where . . . . gentlewomen may be instructed in the principles of religion, and . . . . in all things taught in other schools. As, work of all sorts, dancing, musick, singing, writing, keeping accompts; half the time to be spent in these things, the other half to be employed in gaining the Latin and French tongues; and those that please may learn Greek and Hebrew, the Italian and Spanish, in all which this gentlewoman hath a competent knowledge." If time allowed, the curriculum was also to embrace the whole circle of the sciences, including, no doubt, orthography, etymology, and prosody, and such trifles as arithmetic and history.

Shortly after the arrival of Miss Frances Willard in England in 1892, she was discussing with a friend some of the phases of English life. "This is a country," said she, "where man is king; woman, courtier." Another American, Mr. R. G. White, came to a similar conclusion when he wrote, in 1881, "England is a Paradise for men."*

The lack of consideration shewn to women and their interests has seldom received a more convincing illus-

Women's Interests not considered— an illustration. tration than when the Schools Inquiry Commission in 1865 prepared to inquire into the condition of boys' secondary schools only. It reminds one of the French peasant's observation: "Je n'ai pas d'enfants; je n'ai que des filles." Happily the Commissioners themselves were open to conviction; among the Assistant-Commissioners were Messrs. Bryce, Fearon, and Fitch, whose consistent advocacy of girls' education has done yeoman service. Miss Emily Davies and Miss Bostock, backed by such names as Dean Stanley, Rev. F. D. Maurice, Dean Alford, Dr. James Martineau, Lord Houghton, and Lord Lingen, petitioned that girls should not be passed over, and the Commissioners granted their prayer.

The inquiry elicited that girls' schools lagged far

Results of Inquiry into Girls' Secondary Education, 1865-67. behind boys', poor as these often were; that they were too small, ill-distributed, expensive and wasteful of energy to cover the ground and produce results

* *England Without and Within.* Boston.

co-extensive even with the efforts put forth. Mr. (now Sir J.) Fitch reported that schoolmistresses were in the habit of speaking slightingly of mental cultivation before their pupils, setting before them as the great aim of life to be attractive and to make conquests ; he alludes to the convenient assumption by some women teachers* that the foundation of the moral character is somehow an alternative to the improvement of the understanding ; they themselves preferring the former. Mr. James Bryce deprecates in his report the use of lamentable catechisms ; and states that the great need is to make parents believe that it is "not to refinement and modesty that a cultivated intelligence is opposed, but to vapidity and languor, and vulgarity of mind, to the love of gossip and love of dress." Mr. Fearon dwells on the shortcomigs of schoolmistresses ; their want of breadth and accuracy of scholarship ; their want of knowledge of the art of instructing a class. He also alludes to the multiplicity of subjects, and the want of systematic physical education. Other Commissioners had a similar story to tell, so that there was ample justification for the general report issued upon girls' schools. They were

The General Report. characterized by "want of thoroughness and foundation ; want of system ; slovenliness and showy superficiality ; inattention to rudiments ; undue time given to accomplishments, and these not taught intelligently, or in any scientific

* Such assumptions were not monopolized by women, men commonly made them also.

manner; want of organization." The report added that these defects, needless to observe, applied to a great extent to boys' education.

At this time, few schools were doing anything like efficient work; what the Commissioners describe was very general. A few honourable ex-

Several Efficient Schools.

ceptions were two girls' colleges in London, Queen's and Bedford. They had been founded for the higher education of women, but were themselves obliged to undertake secondary work, to lay the foundations on which they desired to build. Bedford College had for fifteen years a secondary school attached to it; Queen's College retained the position of a secondary school. Besides these were the North London Collegiate School under Miss F. M. Buss, and the Ladies' College, Cheltenham, of which Miss Beale had been principal since 1858. Miss Buss and Miss Emily Davies gave valuable evidence before the Schools Inquiry Commission in 1865; Miss Beale followed in 1866.

The Commission distinguished three grades of schools in its report: third, second, first, in which education

Grades distinguished by the Schools Inquiry Commission.

terminated at about fourteen, sixteen, and eighteen years of age respectively, the last taking its pupils up to the gate of the universities. The great Commission marks an epoch in Secondary Education. It is true the State has done little to evoke order, yet it has been compelled to do something, and other forces have been at work to raise the standard. The Oxford Conference of 1893 and the Royal Commission of 1894–95 both agree that the recommendation of the Schools Inquiry Commissioners to create Third Grade schools has become obsolete. The Higher Grade elementary schools are taking the place these might have occupied, and are slowly wiping out a certain class of inefficient secondary schools. Two grades only of Secondary Education are necessary: First Grade preparing students for the universities, and ending at eighteen or nineteen ; Second Grade schools, where education does not proceed so far, ending at about sixteen.

In the paper she read at the Oxford Conference, Mrs. Bryant only distinguished High schools and **High Schools** Middle schools for girls. The terms **and Middle** suffer from vagueness, largely because **Schools.** a goodly number of girls' schools assume the more pretentious title without any right. The best test for a High school would be the ability of its upper students to pass at once to a College of University rank, and prepare for an Honour degree. A fair proportion of High school students are usually able to take the Cambridge and Oxford Senior Examinations at the honours limit of age. A Middle school, on the other hand, may be expected not to carry its pupils of sixteen or thereabouts much beyond the standard of the Oxford and Cambridge Junior Examinations ; and these they may take when beyond the honours limit of age (below sixteen for a junior).

It has been already stated that we owe Free Trade

in education to the Reformation. It introduced the
era of exaggerated individualism. As

Free Trade in Education.
early as 1179, Dr. Schaible reminds
us, a Lateran Council directed that
the head teacher of every cathedral was to have
authority over all other schoolmasters in his district,
to have the right of license to teach, and without that
license none was to presume to teach. The Church
of Rome, therefore, enunciated the principle with great
clearness ; the Church of England did her best to
prevent all teaching save that by her own members ;
the State, the legitimate heir of the Church in all
matters educational, has never taken up the position
she indicated. This has led to serious disorganization,
to confusion worse confounded in Secondary Education.
It is not too much to say that the absence of registration for the profession is a humiliation to all properly-
qualified teachers. The drug-seller and the horse-doctor
have for years required diplomas ; any charlatan may
open a secondary school by means of a specious
prospectus, and even a bogus degree, and impose on
the credulity of the British parent. Possessed of no
standards by which to test education, "Live and let
live" seems to him a suitable motto even for so serious
a matter as his child's education. At the moment of
writing (January, 1897), the fault that there exists no
teachers' register lies partly with the teachers them-

A Double Register or a Single.
selves, a section of those engaged in
secondary teaching objecting to a
single register for all the teachers of

the country, including those of public elementary schools; and partly with the present Government, who in 1896 introduced an Education Bill. It provided for the registration of teachers, but contained contentious matter which led to the withdrawal of the Bill in July, 1896. The registration difficulty, so far as the fault lies with teachers, is an outcome of the low status of English elementary teachers previous to 1870. In Scotland the teacher has, from time immemorial, been held in honour, ranking only after the minister of the parish; and sometimes teaching whilst awaiting an appointment in the Church of Scotland. It is more of a principle with the Scottish people to sacrifice the quality of food and clothing than to sacrifice education. In England, other traditions and standards have prevailed. Allusion is made

Position of the Teacher in England and Scotland compared.
elsewhere to the fact that the failures of trades and handicrafts took to teaching in the elementary schools as the last resource. A marked improvement in the status of the elementary teacher has taken place of recent years. A certain style of man and woman still needs weeding out if teachers are to be, as they ought to be, a great missionary force for the next quarter of a century. On the other hand, it is equally true that too large a proportion of secondary teachers are not properly qualified. Although some of the best men teachers are opposed to a single register, all the cream of the profession do not favour a double one. The education and status of the elementary

teacher are better than ever before. The London School Board has in its employ more than a hundred men holding degrees, and four women, besides seventeen holding the L.L.A. of St. Andrews.

Forces that have raised the character of Girls' Secondary Education.

First in point of time, credit must be given to the local examinations, whose influence has been very great.

(a) The Local Examinations. Of late years it has become the fashion in certain quarters to speak slightingly of the effect of examinations upon education; in the opinion of some good authorities they exercise a cramping and confining influence after a certain stage is reached. Probably this opinion took root at a time when syndicates and boards of examiners shewed a tendency to disregard and even resent the advice of practical teachers. University dons, having little connection with the education of the young, adopted rigid rules and methods, seldom associating with themselves active, vigorous teachers, whose more recent experience should have proved valuable. Happily this tendency is quite of the past; there is probably no board of examiners working to-day that would not hear and weigh a suggestion of any value. The College of Preceptors makes part of its modern languages examination oral; and though the innovation is not without attendant disadvantage, the balance of advantage undoubtedly lies on the side of greater care as regards accent and pronunciation.

The College of Preceptors was first in the examination field as far as schools are concerned; in 1850 its council sanctioned a scheme which was completed and adopted in 1854. Mr. C. R. Hodgson states that in 1851 the first girls' school was examined, consisting of thirty-five pupils, of whom two gained higher and five lower certificates. In 1870 only 1517 candidates sat for the College Certificates. From that year onwards progress was very marked, and in 1895 the candidates numbered 16,549, besides 350 teachers seeking diplomas. Of the former number, 7039 were girls, and of the latter, 136 women. The College of Preceptors divides its candidates into four classes: first, second, third, and junior forms. In the first class successful candidates are arranged as "honours" and "pass"; second and third class have each three divisions.

College of Preceptors, 1854.

The University of Oxford established its local examination for boys in 1857, Cambridge following in 1858. In 1862 Miss Emily Davies was secretary to a committee which had been formed to obtain for women admission to the university examinations; the ladies first turned their attention to the local examinations as a convenient point of attack, and by a narrow majority—fifty-five to fifty-one—the Cambridge examinations were formally opened to girls in 1865.*

Oxford and Cambridge Local Examinations, 1857, 1858.

* The Secretary of the Local Examinations Syndicate cautiously consented that extra copies of the examination papers should be printed for the use of girl candidates on December 14th, 1863.

The examinations now cover three classes : preliminary, junior, senior, with an age limit of fourteen, sixteen, nineteen for passing in honours.   Candidates may pass, but not in honours, at ages above those named.   The Cambridge Local Examination has an

Extraordinarily Minute Classification.   extraordinarily minute classification of the candidates, almost equal to a hierarchy.   Thus a junior may pass in IA., IB., II., III. classes of honours ; pass (ordinary) ; pass in English and obligatory subjects only (below 16 years) ; pass beyond this age (equivalent to a lower form of pass, commonly known as senior-junior) ; besides gaining marks of distinction in specific subjects.   Preliminary and senior candidates are similarly classified, except that class I. has no sub-divisions.   The intelligence of parents must surely be taxed to grasp these minute

Cambridge Higher Local, 1868.   sub-divisions.   In 1868 the University instituted a special examination, known as the Cambridge Higher Local, for women over eighteen.   The yearly number of candidates averages about 900.

When the question of opening the Cambridge Examinations to girls was first mooted, some authorities were

The Syndicate could not order examiners to examine girls' papers, but the Ladies' Committee were empowered to make their own terms with them.   The result was a pretty heavy list of failures, but, neither dismayed nor discouraged, the Committee pressed on. In 1864 the Senate of the University of Cambridge received a memorial praying that the examinations be opened to girls, signed by 999 influential names.   As the results of the 1863 examination did not appear to have unsexed the candidates, the Senate discussed the memorial.

of opinion that the standard should be lowered for girls. Happily this was overborne; few things could have had a worse effect upon women's education than the adoption of a double standard, in itself a brand of inferiority. The results have fully justified the course adopted. To mention one subject only, arithmetic. In Mr. Fearon's report in the Commission on Secondary Education, in 1865, he mentions that when the Cambridge Examinations were tentatively opened in 1863, of 13 girls presented by a good private school, 8 failed in arithmetic; out of 25 presented by Miss Buss, 10 failed in the same subject. Indeed, out of a total of forty senior candidates, thirty-four failed in the preliminary arithmetic. A double standard would have undoubtedly meant the lowering of arithmetic. Failures in arithmetic, where the subject is well taught, are rather more common among girls than boys, but not to such an extent as to justify a different standard. The smaller number of girls studying mathematics sufficiently explains this difference between the sexes, and it is only fair to add that there are subjects, such as composition and history, where girls frequently do better than boys, probably because English is more seriously and thoroughly studied in girls' schools.

In this connection it may be well to make an excerpt from the Report of the Oxford and Cambridge Joint Board of Examiners to the Council of the Girls' Public Day School Company in 1887. An examiner writes: "I may say that I was very much astonished at the enormous improvement in the arithmetic of the girls which has taken place in the last ten years. Their arithmetic is now as far in advance of the boys' in style and accuracy as it was then behind."

In 1895 the Universities of Oxford and Cambridge instituted a new examination, the Preliminary, for

Preliminary Examinations, 1895. students below 14, and this has led to a considerable accession in the number of candidates, which, in December of that year, rose, in the case of Cambridge, to 13,587; of this number 5642 were girls. A glance at the Cambridge tables will show that a higher percentage of girls pass than of boys; on the other hand, a higher percentage of boys take honours.

Oxford opened its examinations to girls in 1870. The regulations resemble those of Cambridge, including

Oxford Local Examinations opened to Girls, 1870. the division into three honours classes, with a double pass list distinguishing between those who pass at a given age-limit, and those who are beyond it. The numbers of Oxford candidates have greatly increased of recent years. In July, 1896, there were 7314; 2141 of these were preliminary, 3626 juniors, 1547 seniors. Of the total number 5312 passed. Oxford has also three examinations for women.

Many schools use the matriculation examination of London University to test the work of the higher

London Matriculation. forms. The examinations of Durham are used in theNorth, and now the recently chartered Universities of Victoria and Wales are beginning examination schemes of their own. Oxford reports that 1896 marked a great increase in the number of candidates from elementary schools, especially Higher Grade Board schools. It is probable that since the Education Department is now mainly assessing the Government grant to elementary schools by means of inspection, and discontinuing examination for this purpose, able teachers will more and more have recourse to the testing of their work by some external examination authority, and that such authority will affect the curricula of elementary schools just as it has affected secondary schools.

In at least one substantial particular the great examining bodies for schools (the College of Preceptors,

Syndicate Buildings, Cambridge. the Cambridge Syndicate, and Oxford Delegacy) may congratulate themselves on the adoption of so reasonable a policy as the admission of girls to examination. The handsome buildings of the College of Preceptors, in Bloomsbury Square, are largely due to profits on examination; the Syndicate Buildings, as the present Bishop of Stepney (Canon G. F. Browne) observed, owe existence to the candidates' threepences, wisely husbanded; and even now a building is being erected for the Oxford Delegacy, whose bill will be similarly met.

Of late years, the Universities have provided able examiners, who examine and report upon the whole of a school; and this system is preferred by many teachers to local examinations, since the entire work is thus reviewed.

The examinations of the Oxford and Cambridge Schools Examination Board, usually styled the Joint

Joint Board Examinations, 1873.   Board, founded in 1873, have grown considerably in popularity. The examinations and certificates are of two classes—higher and lower—adapted for different ages; the papers can be worked as part of the examination of a school; it is possible for a candidate so to arrange his subjects that if one year he passes in English, together with subjects selected from two other groups, he may in the following year enter for examination without again taking English. In 1896, the Joint Board examined 96 boys' schools and 69 girls' schools, thirty-two of these belonging to the Girls' Public Day Schools Co. Of the 2121 candidates for the higher certificate 1431 were boys, 690 girls. For the lower certificate there were 891 candidates, 750 boys, 141 girls. Of the 2121 candidates for the higher certificate, 449 had already gained certificates in a previous examination of the Joint Board, and of this number 178 gained a certificate, with distinction, in 1896. Of the girls, 441 were candidates for partial certificates (letters) only; letters were given to 290 girls.

It may be objected that there is too much "preparation" for examinations in certain schools; but, on the other hand, it must be admitted that examinations have put an end to superficiality in girls' schools. Further, they have stimulated the girls, and admitted of a useful comparison between their work and that of boys.

Forces tending to raise the character of Secondary Education.

Second in order of time, though first in point of value, must be placed the work of the Endowed Schools Commission. The Commissioners have been the consistent friends of girls' education, maintaining their right to consideration even when refractory corporations would have passed them over. English legislation is almost invariably a result of public opinion; it scarcely ever leads. For this reason the Commission have not aimed at anything like equality of consideration for the sexes, since public opinion lags behind the natural division of educational benefits.

(*b*) **The Charity Commission.**

The Endowed Schools Acts are the one practical result of the Schools Inquiry Commission which sat from 1865–1867. The recent Royal Commission upon Secondary Education styles the report of that Commission epoch-making, luminous, and exhaustive. Though its important recommendations as regards a Central Authority, a Local or Provincial Authority, a Central Council of Education—recommendations, be it observed, which, after the lapse of 30 years, the Commission of 1894 could do little more than endorse— were not carried out, women have special cause for gratitude that the outcome was beneficial to their interests. Parliament passed the first Endowed Schools Act, introduced by Mr. W. E. Forster, in 1869, and as a result the Endowed Schools Commission was created. At first the Commission was nominated for a limited period; since 1874 it has been a department of the Charity Commission.

During these years, out of nearly 2000 educational endowments known to be within the jurisdiction of the **Girls admitted to** Endowed Schools Acts, the Com- **the benefits of** missioners have framed schemes for **Endowments.** 902 endowments, besides constantly amending those which grew obsolete or proved unworkable. About 80 of these schemes refer to girls. Large numbers of schools reformed of themselves, and the presence of a good endowed school in a neighbourhood caused the private schools to adopt the pace set by the Commission. Public interest in education, languid as it too often is, was aroused by the introduction to governing bodies of a large and increasing representative element, which has been helpful in forming local opinion. Besides which, the Commissioners established an organic relation between schools and local government authorities. Their policy will doubtless pave the way for a local educational authority, which is greatly needed, but for which some parts of the country are not ready.

The numbers attending endowed schools have greatly increased, as a result of wise administration. In 1865 Harpur's Foundation at Bedford maintained 799 boys; in 1893 there were 1445 boys and 666 girls. The quality of the education, needless to say, is very different.

There were four ways open to the Commissioners to benefit girls :—

(*a*) The establishment of girls' schools.
(*b*) Exhibitions for girls.
(*c*) Power to benefit girls when the endowment suffices for the purpose.
(*d*) The admission of girls to boys' schools.

All these ways were adopted, but *d* is the most rare. The term "endowed school" is somewhat loose ; any school is endowed that has had so little as its site given. It is chiefly used for schools where certain moneys have been set apart for maintenance. The Charity Commission have no funds at their disposal for the endowment of education ; their function is to regulate and supervise public trusts. The Commissioners **City Companies** have on several occasions recom-**and the claims** mended wealthy city companies to **of Girls.** spend accumulated funds on the education of girls. The Skinners, Brewers, Clothworkers, Haberdashers, Merchant Taylors, Drapers, Leather-sellers, and Goldsmiths have devoted large sums to this object. The main idea actuating Commissioners has been to obtain for girls a sound, broad, general education, differentiating little from that given to boys, save in one or two technical subjects like sewing. Amongst the best known schools for which they have provided schemes are the North London Collegiate, Manchester High School for Girls, Birmingham Grammar Schools, Stamford (Lincs.), and the Bradford Grammar

School.   The proportion in which the funds of an
endowment are divided between girls and boys is
determined mainly by the locality and by public
opinion.   The commonest division is a third to girls,
two-thirds to boys.

Those who have looked into the history of endowments soon perceive two main tendencies: the rich

**Tendencies of
Endowments.**

acquire what was meant for the poor;
boys what was left to children.   One
explanation suffices: the poor and
women were not represented on Boards of Governors.
The Charity Commissioners, on the grounds that all
resources must be used, and that it would be hard to
maintain that many women are not admirably qualified,
have, in their schemes for girls, required that a certain
number of women shall act as Governors.

In a country like England, much that affects the
public weal is subject to constant criticism.   The

**Endowments are
increasing.**

statement has been made that the
race of pious founders would die out
when it was seen that benefactions
were overhauled and rearranged at the mercy of Commissioners.   In their 42nd report a crushing retort to
this criticism will be found.   Charitable trusts are
increasing to the extent of 500 yearly.   From 1875
to 1894, reckoning only gifts of £1000 and upwards,
£8,000,000 was bequeathed to seven principal objects,
education and medical relief obtaining the largest
amounts.   Paragraph 10 concludes thus:—" Indeed,
there is reason to think that the latter half of the 19th

century will stand second, in respect of the greatness and variety of the charities created within its duration, to no other half-century since the Reformation. And, as to one particular branch of educational endowments, namely, that for the advancement of the secondary and superior education of girls and women, it may be anticipated that future generations will look back to the period immediately following upon the Schools Inquiry Commission, and the consequent passing of the Endowed Schools Acts, as marking an epoch in the creation and application of endowments for that branch of education, similar to that which is marked for the education of boys and men by the Reformation."

Forces tending to raise the character of Secondary Education.

The passing of the great Education Acts, marking a new era in the annals of this country, indirectly (*c*) **Elementary Education Act, 1870.** affected private schools by wiping out many of the inferior sort, used by the lower middle classes. A better education could be obtained in a good Board school, under certificated teachers, than from some private schoolmistresses, whose sole qualification was often the "selectness" of their establishments, which seemed, according to the door-plate, to be universally attended by "young ladies." It has already been shown how, during recent years, necessity has compelled public elementary schools to enlarge their curricula for sixth, seventh, and extra-standard classes, and sometimes to build separate schools, under the name of Higher Grade schools. Another kind of school has also arisen, partly as a result of improved Elementary Education and the stimulus that has recently been given to Technical Education. These are the Organized Science schools, working mainly under the Science and Art Department to secure its grants. Their numbers increased from 132 in 1895, to 152 in 1896, and they educate almost 19,000 students, of whom 4000 are girls.

In the sixties and seventies may be observed a large number of educational associations rising over the (d) **Girls' Public** country, of which a goodly proportion **Day School** concerned themselves with women's **Company.** education. The North of England Council for promoting the Higher Education of Women is fairly well known, since by its invitation in 1867 to Prof. James Stuart, to give a course of lectures to ladies at Leeds, Liverpool, Manchester, and Sheffield, it assisted to lay the foundation of the University Extension movement. The Yorkshire Ladies' Council of Education dates from 1865, when ladies began to superintend the Cambridge Local Examinations in the West Riding, newly opened to girls. Its branches undertook educational work in various towns. In 1871 was formed a National Union for Improving the Education of Women, amongst whose founders were Mrs. Wm. Grey, and her sister Miss Shirreff, with Princess Louise as president. The Union meant business; an arch-Conservative was so impressed by the fact that he alluded to it as a "widely-ramifying conspiracy." The first thing it did was to publish a monthly paper: *The Women's Educational Journal.* In January, 1873, the Girls' Public Day School Company, incorporated in June, 1872, another outcome of this union for improving women's education, opened its first school at Chelsea. The National Union also undertook to provide means for the training of teachers; and for this purpose the Maria Grey Training College for Secondary Teachers was founded in 1878, although by that time this special work had passed into the hands of the Teachers' Training and Registration Society.

The Girls' Public Day School Company has, from the first, been a paying concern : its shareholders have religiously touched a yearly dividend of five per cent. Profits over and above this amount are devoted to the improvement of the schools. As far as numbers are concerned, success can hardly be regarded as phenomenal, for in 1896 the schools only numbered 36, with about 7200 pupils. Yet their effect has been far-reaching, so that we may not refuse to call the result **The Schools have** admirable. The schools have shewn **created a** how high a standard we may reason- **Standard.** ably expect of girls of the middle class ; how useful is discipline ; how girls can disregard the class distinctions which were once thought to be so peculiarly beneficial to the feminine mind and morals. In the mistresses of these High Schools, both head and assistant, we have seen a new type of woman evolved, highly educated, exerting great moral force, ruling with justice and kindness. Women are sometimes told that they cannot co-operate : a well-managed High School shews whether the statement is borne out by facts. The Church Schools Company followed in 1883, with definite Church teaching as a main article of its constitution. Its schools number 24 ; pupils about 2000. The effect of the Girls' Public Day Schools upon private schools can hardly be exaggerated ; on all hands it is admitted to be very great. The fees are usually, with extras, from £9 9s. to £15 15s. per annum, according to age, the lack of endowment prohibiting low fees. It is therefore evident that the schools are for persons in comfortable circumstances. They cannot be used by those who have large British families numbering half a score, if of the lower middle class. For them, in the main, no adequate provision exists, or ever has existed. The low standard of culture, or to speak plainly, the absence of culture which marks the English lower middle classes, is thus sufficiently explained. As a rule, little is expected of girls of this class of life, and less than little is obtained.

Forces tending to raise the character of Secondary Education.

A fifth great force which has tended to improve the character of Secondary Education is the education and (e) **Improved Education of Women Teachers.** training of the teachers themselves, by no means the least of the forces enumerated. The great lack of the Government, when it first made money grants for

Elementary Education, was that of suitable teachers; it knew not where to turn to find them. The same lack existed in Secondary Education. To-day the women's colleges are turning out hundreds of well-educated women; the training colleges send forth scores of both educated and trained teachers. Unhappily their very numbers prevent them getting their due reward; there is too much reason to state that improved and even excellent education has not favourably affected the woman teacher in the labour market. A graduate of London University would seem to have almost as much difficulty in securing the very modest reward of £100 per annum as her slenderly educated sister of a previous generation.

The Royal Commission of 1894–95 marks the second great epoch in Secondary Education, just as the Schools

Royal Commission on Secondary Education of 1894-95. Inquiry Commission marked the first. It is too early to speak of its effects; its important recommendations still require legislation. We may note that of its seventeen members, three were women: Dr. Sophie Bryant, Lady F. Cavendish, and Mrs. Henry Sidgwick. Moreover, of the fourteen Assistant Commissioners, five were women. For this reason, amongst others, the interests of their sex were carefully considered; so much so that no complaint on the subject has yet been heard. The Commission commented upon the great improvement in girls' education by means of endowed and proprietary schools; regretted that, owing to the backward state of public opinion, the Charity

Commission had not been able to make a more equal division of the funds at its disposal ; alluded to the fact that girls get an unequal share of technical instruction —in some cases being even excluded—and also to the constant, one might say the growing need of scholarships and exhibitions to pass girls on to the universities. The report, with its repeated cry for organization, is too recent to allow of lengthy extracts from its valuable recommendations.   Never before have purely educational matters aroused so much public interest ; the Act of 1870 inflamed the passions of religious bigotry, which has happily never been an element in Secondary Education.   The press, after the publication of the Report in October, 1895, commented largely, and on the whole intelligently, on the problems which had been dealt with.   A large number of conferences quickly followed.   It was not uncommon for ladies in the audience to bring their blue-book with them and anxiously scan its pages for the special point which the speaker was discussing.

Since the passing of the Education Act of 1870, the Welsh have made extraordinary progress in edu-

Welsh Intermediate Education Act, 1889.

cation, both elementary, secondary, and higher.   In the organization of Secondary Education, they have really led the way, owing, doubtless, to the fact that in Wales the ground was less covered than in England.   The Principality, with which is grouped Monmouth, is distinguished by a great love of knowledge.   There are miners acquainted with the higher mathematics, servants and labourers who compose essays and poems for the Eisteddfod. Aberystwyth College, opened in 1862, was largely subscribed for in small sums by persons of humble means. The Welsh people tried to interest the Government in their educational difficulties, especially the almost entire lack of good Secondary Education, and succeeded in obtaining the appointment of a Departmental Committee of Inquiry in 1880, consisting of half a dozen men well qualified for the task. The Committee began to sit in 1881, and held meetings in London and Wales. They rapidly produced a valuable report, shewing the existing state of Secondary Education, drawing special attention to the absence of educational opportunities for girls, and making recommendations. As a result, Parliament passed the Welsh Intermediate Education Act in 1889, since which time 70 secondary schools have been opened in Wales and Monmouth. Men of acknowledged ability assisted to

Each Welsh County or County-Borough has a Scheme. carry out the scheme; the scheme for each county is the joint work of an Education Committee and of the Charity Commissioners, who throughout lent valuable assistance. The county, or a borough of 50,000, was taken as the unit, each county having its own committee, composed of three members appointed by the County Council and two by the Lord President of the Council. Each committee was entitled to draw up its own scheme; but as a series of conferences were arranged between all the different committees, differences are fewer than might have been expected,

H

and may be said simply to mark varying local needs. The committees had the services of an officer of the Charity Commissioners, whose wide experience in educational matters was valuable, and tended to minimise unnecessary variety.

If we turn to the consideration of how these schools are financed, we find that finance is the cause of their greatest difficulty and anxiety, tending to hamper their development and efficiency. It will be remembered that in 1890 a considerable sum of money had been raised for the compensation of publicans on the extinction of their licences. Popular opinion was strongly opposed to such a use of the public funds, and happily the sum has been devoted to educational purposes. The Welsh secured the right of applying their share of this money to the purposes of the Intermediate Education Act, the sum amounting to about £30,000 annually. In addition, Wales rated herself to the extent of ½d. in the pound for the same object, producing in this way £15,500. The Imperial Treasury makes a yearly grant of like amount, conditional on efficiency maintained; and this, with about £20,000 representing the annual value of Welsh scholastic endowments dealt with by schemes under the Acts, gives a total of about £80,000 per annum. The sum is too small when we consider the number of schools that must share in it. It does not admit of the teachers being sufficiently well paid, and in some cases prevents a sufficient number of teachers being employed. To increase the number

Finance a difficulty.

of their scholars many schools have reduced their fees. The result has been large additions to numbers, without a corresponding addition to the financial prosperity of the school. The scholars in many

Practical proof of interest in Education. schools only pay for one half the education they receive, the Governors providing the other half. The Welsh people have shewn generosity towards these schools. Probably £100,000, including the value of the sites presented, has been subscribed towards the buildings. A small and poor district, on the borders of Caermarthen and Cardigan, with a population of 15,000, collected £2000 for its intermediate school. Many others have subscribed between £1000 and £2000, so great is their energy and enthusiasm, their belief in education. " The English," said an educationist, observing these things, " would think you lunatic to ask for what the Welsh have done."

The Welsh schemes find places for about 5000 boys and 3000 girls, or for 6 per 1000 of the population. The smaller number of the girls must be taken to mean a smaller demand on the part of parents for the education of their daughters. Had the demand been equal for both sexes, probably the supply of places would have been so also. It is satisfactory to note that the demand on the part of the girls is increasing. The Cardiff Girls' School now numbers 184 pupils ; Swansea, 226.*

* The Swansea School has now begun technical evening classes for outsiders in such subjects as cookery, dressmaking, laundry, nursing, gymnastics.

The effect of the organization of Welsh Intermediate Education has been the disappearance of many small and inefficient private schools. In some cases the Committee took over schools they found in existence, and sometimes teachers, and used them in their scheme.

Effects of Organization.

᾿ In the governing bodies of the schools the scheme has arranged that a minimum number of governors shall be women; in several cases the minimum has been exceeded. A difficulty has been met occasionally in dual schools, that of the mistress in charge of the girls' department having to work under the head-master. Probably the dual system will only be temporary: as time goes on, the schools will either become separate or mixed. The dual system was adopted because of poverty, small schools being always proportionately expensive.

The Welsh experiment is highly interesting to educationists. There can be no doubt that when England proceeds to the development of a scheme of Secondary Education, the experience of Wales will be valuable and suggestive

It was in 1832 that a modest grant of £20,000 was first voted in Parliament to be applied to educational purposes. Three years later we find a Select Committee of the House of Commons, on the motion of Mr. William Ewart, M.P. for Liverpool, appointed "to inquire into the best means of extending a knowledge of the arts and of the principles of design among

Science and Art Department, 1837.

the people (especially the manufacturing population) of the country." In 1836 the sum of £1500 was set aside for a Normal School of Design with a museum and lectures; and, in 1837, the School of Design was constituted. It was the beginning of the magnificent collection of art treasures at South Kensington, and of that department whose relations to the Education Department remain to the mere lay mind a bewildering and intricate tangle. It was supposed that the Education Bill, introduced by Sir John Gorst in the House of Commons, was intended to unravel some of the complex mysteries that have arisen in course of time, but the withdrawal of the Bill in July, 1896, has deferred a rearrangement which the course of time, growth, and fresh developments in both departments have rendered an absolute necessity. In 1852 a Department of Practical Art was created to supersede the Schools of Design, which were not satisfactory; in 1853 the Science division was added; in 1856 the Education Department was constituted, and both it and the Science

Education Department constituted, 1856. and Art Department, were placed under the control of the Lord President of the Council and the Vice-President of the Committee of Council on Education. The extension and reconstitution of the Science and Art Department were largely owing to the chagrin of the English on perceiving that their exhibits in the Great International Exhibition of 1851 were inferior in taste and originality to those of Continental nations, especially the French. Like the Education Department, South Kensington, as it is popularly called, has seen many changes. These include its location—for it began at Somerset House—its constitution, aims, and methods; it has grown to its present dimensions in true English fashion, and, on the whole, may lay claim to a fair amount of adaptability.

Its work may be summed up as follows :—

1. Its main and original work, the holding of science and art evening classes all over the country, the **Functions of the** initiative depending chiefly upon local **Science and Art** effort. Art classes naturally came to **Department.** be held by day as well as in the evening.

2. The Royal College of Art in London, the centre for all art schools over the country, and in which, to a large extent, art teachers are trained.

3. The Royal College of Science, holding a similar position to science classes of the Department held in the country.

4. The School of Mines in Jermyn Street.

5. Organized Science schools, a sort of Higher Grade school in their relation to Elementary Education. These are growing very rapidly. They numbered 132 in 1895; 152 in 1896. At present the students number almost 19,000, of whom about 4000 are girls. School Boards and other bodies earning the grants of the Department usually conduct an experiment in co-education in these Science schools.

The Estimates for 1896–97 granted £727,000 for the expenditure at South Kensington. Until recently it took little share in organizing and directing educational work, but paid out a money grant by means of examinations held yearly in April and May. The Department first adopted the system known as "payment by results," which most authorities consider to

Payment by Results.

have a depressing effect upon the teaching power, and a cramping one upon the scholar. It may reasonably be doubted whether any better system has ever been invented, for most other systems seem only able to work well on the assumption that all teachers are able, conscientious, and energetic. Unhappily, this is assuming too much. Already teachers can tell of subordinates relaxing vigour since payment by results has been superseded, and some head-masters and mistresses begin to perceive that grant now falleth on the just and the unjust alike.

The elasticity of the Department is commendable. There is much freedom in subjects; work in the remotest village may be recognized and paid by the Department. Save on the art side, classes have not been largely used by girls, with the exception of subjects like botany and physiology. Local initiative, or the lack of it, must be blamed for this, for the Department itself is generally guiltless of the stupidity of making unnecessary sex distinctions. Classes in connection with South Kensington, to the number of 7000 or 8000, are held all over the country, from Thurso to Penzance. The teaching depends on what is available; what the man on the spot can give to his neighbour-

hood. With few exceptions, chiefly the post of assistant-
teacher in Schools of Art, or mistress in an organized
Science school, the work of teaching under South
Kensington does not seem to commend itself to
women, either because they are unenterprising, un-
suited for it, or fail to commend themselves to local
committees. Perhaps if more women sat on such
committees, the case would be different.

For 1896 the Department has set on foot considerable changes. Payment by results is to recede still
Recent Changes. further; and now a somewhat complicated system, partly depending on
fixed payment by attendance, so much for each
attendance, and partly depending on efficiency, to be
tested by inspection and the result of examinations, has
been instituted. The Department has aimed by this
means at the saving of rural and semi-rural schools.
The work done in great centres of population like Leeds
and Birmingham is sometimes of university standard;
in country places it is usually elementary. For the
latter to compete with the former, simply spelt
destruction of rural effort. For this reason the new
system has been adopted; and whether success ensues
or failure, praise is due to the Department for its
attempt to nurse rural districts. In many country
places where the squire and parson are supreme, education is at a very low ebb. In a quiet way, they back
up local apathy; and the absence of a middle class
contributes to maintain things as they are.

Another change worth chronicling is the hour at

which the spring examinations are held. Usually these
have been held between 7 and 10 p.m.; but in 1897
alternative examinations will be held in the afternoon.
In Organized Science schools, the amount of time
devoted to science has been reduced from fifteen to
thirteen hours per week; a certain proficiency in
literature has been required of students in advanced or
higher courses; the number of inspectors has been
increased, and in a small proportion of cases the money
grant has been given on the result of inspection of the
whole school, rather than on individual achievement.
The changes in the schools were not made compulsory
for the first year, but afterwards the fixed grant will
depend partly upon attendance, as in the evening classes
of the Department. These changes really mark a
revolution in the methods of South Kensington. Up
to the present time, the aim may be said to have been
the strengthening of the strong; henceforth the weak
will receive more attention.

Besides its system of examinations, by which the
value of the work is appraised, numbers of drawings,
National paintings, models, studies, designs, are
Competition at sent up yearly to South Kensington
South Kensington. from Schools of Art and Art Classes
all over the country. More than 88,000 of these were
sent up in 1896; of this number, 4398 were selected
for national competition. These selected works of art
form an interesting exhibition in a suite of South
Kensington rooms, where they are every year on view
to the public during the month of August. In the

opinion of the officials, girls and women hold their own.

Ou: of eleven students to whom a gold medal was awarded in 1896, three were girls. In the section devoted to the National Training at South Kensington, the only gold medallist (honorary) was a woman. Mr. Walter Crane observed of this competition, far too little visited by the British parent: "The Department may fairly ask whether any other country could make so creditable and interesting a show in so many branches of design."

In Great Britain there are now altogether 225 Schools of Art, with 67 branches, and 1448 art classes, with the **Local Schools** handsome total of 136,000 students. **of Ar:.** It has been already shewn how drawing is compulsory for boys in public elementary schools; in 1894 South Kensington had 2,100,000 pupils in the State schools, for whose instruction it made grants. The Department very properly lays great stress upon local effort; probably foreigners visiting our country and commenting upon our institutions, are apt to over-estimate local zeal. The Department presupposes and requires it, in order to work well; where it has failed most, such zeal has not existed. Three large towns in Norfolk and Suffolk together earned in 1892–93, £2690; the rest of the counties, with a population four times greater, earned £729.

It is worth while noting that in October, 1896, a committee was appointed to inquire into the distribution of the grants of the Science and Art Department; of its six members, one is Mrs. Henry Sidgwick, Principal of Newnham College.

Beside the educational work of the Polytechnics, the classes under County Councils, and the University Extension movement, dealt with in the next section, there is in England a notable development in the popular education of adults, which can only be conveniently classified here. It is partly educational, but largely social and recreative in addition. France is about to reorganize secondary instruction for adults, a result of two important social congresses held at Le Havre and Bordeaux. M. F. Buisson came to London to see what was being done on this side of the Channel, and has published a book on his observations, including monographs by the men and women at work in the movement.* The beginnings of adult education for the working classes are traced to Anderson, Black, and to Dr. George Birkbeck, the founders of Mechanics' Institutes, now numbering about 2000 in Britain. The earliest courses of evening lectures for artizans seem to have been started at Glasgow. We have seen how this movement slipped back for want of elementary education; but the idea it embodies is too characteristic of the Saxon race not to reappear in many ways. "The first impulse of a Huxley, a Tyndall," says M. Emil Boutmy, "is to popularize their work." This altruistic spirit calls itself religious, or philanthropic, or educational,

Marginal note: Adult Secondary Education.

---

* *L'éducation populaire des adultes en Angleterre; de M. F. BUISSON. Hachette, 1896.

or social; but it is one and the same, and causes those who know us to admit that we are the most essentially democratic and social of all the great nations, despite, and to some extent because of, our terrible extremes of wealth and poverty. It shows itself in another form in the University Settlements now to be found in London and other great cities. Of these, there are now ten in the capital. They mark the growth of the idea that culture, refinement, education are not for the few, but for all. Toynbee is one of the oldest and most

Toynbee Hall a typical Settlement. typical of the settlements. Canon Barnett strongly objects to Toynbee being styled a mission or an educational centre,; he prefers to call it a club. We shall find there from 1000 to 1500 students or members attracted to the club for one reason or another. Canon Barnett is of opinion that about one-third of these are women. Related to the settlements are the Social Institutes, now numbering four in London, and a host of clubs whose aims are social, moral, and educative. Gymnastics, music, the æsthetic sense, hygiene are more or less cultivated in most of them, besides the encouragement of thrift, and fostering of friendly relations between members of the aristocracy, of privilege, wealth, and culture, and Society's workers. No city in the world can show such degradation—physical, mental, and moral—as London; the curse of the poor is indeed his poverty. But neither can any city show such efforts to bridge the great gulf between the privileged and unprivileged classes. The whole movement has well been styled the secondary education of the working classes.

The offices of the National Home Reading Union are situated in Surrey House, Victoria Embankment. The Union has a membership of more than 8000—too **The National** small, considering the excellence of **Home-reading** its work. Its object is to stimulate, **Union.** encourage, and direct home reading in such a way as to make it educational in the truest sense of the word. It seeks to give home reading definiteness, continuity, and system, adapting itself to suit the wants of all ages, classes, and degrees of culture and development. The work is done by means of local branches, or circles, as well as by larger organizations, such as literary or scientific institutes, co-operative societies, and labour unions. Naturally the success of the Union depends largely on the zeal and enthusiasm of the local circle leaders or secretaries ; unhappily these must largely be sought among teachers and other busy persons, whose hands are already full.

The circles are usually formed among three chief classes : boys and girls who have left the elementary schools, and whose reading needs direction ; artizans whose tastes incline to a certain measure of culture ; and a third class, of the omnibus kind, embracing all sorts and conditions of men and women. Culture, not class, is the standard of the Union. Men and women who have been to the university accept its guidance in their special studies. Pupil teachers look to it for direction as to the best and cheapest books bearing upon their work. Board school managers accept its hints as to methods of awakening interest in intellectual life after leaving school.

The Union has special courses in English History, Literature (including Shakspere and Browning courses), Architecture, Greek and Roman History and Literature, French, German, Geography, Ethics, Economic and Social Science, Travel, Natural Science, and other subjects. It is instrumental in inducing publishers to undertake cheap editions of works suitable for its purpose, many thousands of which it causes to be distributed every year. The reading courses are drawn up by eminent educationists, and clearly show that the needs of different classes and ages are understood. The Union, under its capable secretary, Miss Mondy, is adaptable. An instance of this is afforded by its readiness to work in with the recently constituted Evening Continuation schools: a reading circle of the N.H.R.U. may be connected with the schools, and a grant earned on attendance.

Another feature is its summer assembly. In addition to the advantage of companionship in systematic reading, personal help, and stimulus at circle meetings, the N.H.R.U. organizes enjoyable educational summer holidays, when field lectures, excursions, conferences, and social gatherings are arranged. These summer assemblies are held, when possible, in such places as best illustrate the year's work, owing to their possession of historic monuments, or to their offering peculiar facilities for the study of geology, botany, and natural history generally. The purpose of the assembly is to give a vivid and realistic interest in the reading of the year.

Since 1889 assemblies have been held at Blackpool, Weston-super-Mare, Bowness, Ilkley, Salisbury, Buxton, Leamington, and, in 1896, at Chester.

In all that has been written upon Secondary Education up to this point, only the explored portions of the territory, the oases of the desert, have been briefly examined. It is a sound axiom to proceed from the known to the unknown, but here it necessarily leads to vagueness. Figures scarcely exist with regard to Secondary Education in general ; no inquiry has ever been instituted to cover the whole of England. The Royal Commissioners of 1894–95 instituted a comparison between three great endowed schools, as they were in 1864 and 1893. The selected schools were Harpur's Foundation at Bedford, the Manchester Grammar School, and King Edward VI.'s Schools at Birmingham. All three had greatly improved, especially if we consider the share given to girls in the endowments. At Birmingham 590 boys were being educated in 1864; the numbers had increased to 1366 boys and 1068 girls in 1893. But this is, of course, explored territory. No doubt the majority of English girls now receiving secondary education obtain it at home, or more commonly, in the private schools. Of these, no accurate survey covering the whole of the country has ever been made. The most important conclusions of the Schools Inquiry

Unexplored Land.

Commissioners, based upon eight selected districts, have already been detailed.

The Commission of 1894–95 allotted seven districts to their Assistant Commissioners ; and there is no reason

Private Schools improving.

to suppose that what is true of these districts does not apply to the whole of England. The number of private schools, both day and boarding, is variously estimated at from 10,000 to 15,000. These are of almost every variety of excellence and miserable inefficiency. "The worst type of private school is rarer than it was 30 years ago," says the Report; "yet the general result of our inquiries has been to show that a large proportion of these schools are unsatisfactory." Some inefficient schools continue to exist because of such reasons as "lower fees, adaptation of the curriculum to the ideas of parents, laxity in enforcing attendance, or supposed social selectness." The Commissioners are of opinion that the private schools have improved since 1869; there are more of the better ones, fewer of the bad ones than formerly. Yet there still are "private schools which, carried on in ill-ventilated rooms by ignorant persons with no qualifications as teachers, represent the lowest depth of educational stagnation from which we have, during the past thirty years, been emerging."

A few years ago some educationists frankly talked

Private Schools and initiation of Educational Reforms.

of sweeping private schools out of existence. It has been said that some of the Commissioners began their work with a strong prejudice against the private schools, and ended it with the conviction that there was much to be said in their favour. It was brought home to their minds that several great educational reforms had been initiated in private schools, and that able and enthusiastic teachers sometimes leave public schools and take to private ones because of the gain in freedom and elasticity. Germany, France, and the United States are now calling out for private schools. "It is possible," says the Report, "so to order the conditions of educational life as to secure at once the freedom of the teacher and the protection of the public."

The Commissioners made recommendations which it is believed will attain this end. Despite the extraordinary proposals that some witnesses made to the Commission, such as that public authorities should be prevented giving any pecuniary support whatever to public secondary schools, which they did not give to efficient private ones, lest the latter should be handicapped, private teachers as a whole will welcome reasonable control by the State ; hardly any assume the attitude of certain German and French educational reformers, who demand the abolition of all State interference. There is a growing agreement with Dr. Schaible's view, published as early as 1870, that the best machinery for the thorough and general instruction of the nation is the equilibrium of three forces: a system of State schools, endowed schools, and private schools.

Visit to Four Secondary Schools for Girls.

The North London Collegiate School, the pioneer public school for girls in England, requires more than **The North London Collegiate School.** mere mention. It was originally begun in 1850 by Frances Mary Buss and her mother, as a private school, in Camden Town. Two years before, Miss Buss had attended evening classes at the newly founded Queen's College, in Harley-street. When the London Centre for the Cambridge Local Examinations was tentatively opened to girls, in 1863, Miss Davies being the secretary, Miss Buss was represented by twenty-five candidates out of a total of 84. Official recognition of the importance and high promise of the new school was not withheld, for in November, 1865, Miss Davies and Miss Buss were called to give evidence before the Royal Commission on Secondary Education. In her book, *Frances Mary Buss,** Miss Ridley shows how from this time forward the idea grew in Miss Buss's mind of making her school into a public school for girls. In 1870 the trust deed was signed by several old friends and other influential persons, amongst them four women. Then followed the hard struggle to find the money to build and endow the new public school. Few stories are so moving in the history of women's education as the grave difficulties Miss Buss encountered. No one realizing that struggle could ever again look with indifferent eye upon the handsome buildings of the

* Published by Longmans, Green, and Co., 1896.

North London Collegiate School. Miss Ridley tells us "There were rare tears in Miss Buss's voice and eyes" when Miss Ewart gave £1000, afterwards supplementing the gift by a timely loan. Success came at last, for in 1872 two great city companies came to the rescue. The Brewers gave £40,000 to build and endow the school; the Clothworkers followed with an offer to build the great hall and an annual grant of £105 for scholarships. Miss Buss herself gave £1000, the profits she gained by supervising a preparatory school, about £1500 to build the gymnasium, as well as sacrificing additional income from the Board of Governors, which should have been hers by right.

This first Public School for Girls was opened by the Prince and Princess of Wales, in 1879, and for **First Public Day** fifteen years Miss Buss remained its **School for Girls,** head-mistress, a period long enough **opened 1879.** to allow her to reap a high reward, and to show the educational world that a great step forward had been taken. The North London Collegiate School served as a model for the Girls' Public Day School Company. It is worked under a scheme drawn up by the Charity Commissioners in 1875, which scheme also covers the Camden School for Girls.

Together the two schools educate about a thousand pupils. The North London Collegiate School, of which Dr. Sophie Bryant is now head-mistress, is a first grade school; the leaving age is about 19, and its students may pass directly into a university college without further preparation. The Camden School is

The Camden School. second grade, the leaving age being 16 or 17, students generally remaining until they pass the Cambridge Junior, or some equivalent examination.

The buildings of the North London Collegiate School are excellent, including a handsome hall with stained glass windows, well furnished class-rooms, laboratories, a large gymnasium, dining-room, and excellent cloak-rooms. Convenience and suitability are the distinguishing features.

In 1879 such buildings were unique; happily, all over the country, and especially in London, buildings quite as good are becoming common, the very result at which Miss Buss aimed. Morning school only obtains, save when pupils choose to remain or return for music and preparation. The Princess of Wales is President of the Board of Governors, on which there are five ladies.

The position of the Cheltenham Ladies' College is unique, if for no other reason than that it covers all

The Ladies' College, Cheltenham. the four sections into which this work is divided. In the main, it is a large secondary school for girls, with some 650 pupils. Its growth has led to important developments in every other field, the scheme now covering secondary, higher, and technico-professional education.

The College began its career in 1854: its principal was a Miss Proctor, succeeded by Miss Beale in 1858. It was then at work in Cambray House, now an over-

flow school of the College. The present College does
not resemble the Royal Holloway College in being the
"result of one act of conception, the successive stages
of a single intellectual effort." It is quite the reverse
of this; building has been added to building, enlargement here, addition there, so that the stranger is
usually bewildered by the variety and number of halls,
rooms, and corridors.

Miss Beale has herself written the history of
Cheltenham College, a story of great interest. Up
to 1873, the year in which the new college buildings
were entered, it was a school of about 150 girls, its
principal having to live down a good deal of local
opposition to a girls' school daring to style itself a
college, and to the heterodox idea that girls need
trouble to make the acquaintance of fractions or
Shakespeare. "It is all very well," Miss Beale re-
lates of a mother who withdrew her daughter at the
end of a quarter of new-fangled tuition, "for my
daughter to read Shakespeare, but don't you think it
is more important for her to sit down at the piano and
amuse her friends?" The great hall of assembly can
contain 600 pupils. A new and larger one is being
built, capable of holding 1500 persons, at a cost of
about £20,000. A handsome museum and library,
laboratories, studios, pictures, statues, statuettes, stained
glass windows, a fine organ, all go to show education
held in high honour.

The staff numbers more than 100; of students,
including those who attend classes as by-students, there

Staff and Pupils. are 900. About 500 pupils live in seventeen boarding-houses licensed by the Council. A point is made that all students shall be daughters of professional men, or those who hold a certain social position.

The College has a kindergarten of about 50 children under trained mistresses, affording practising ground for a Kindergarten Training Department. The remaining 600 students are classed in three great divisions, subdivided into thirty-two classes. The leaving age is seventeen or eighteen, and students are encouraged to take a leaving examination, usually the Oxford Senior; about 70 take this examination in July.

In addition, the College affords preparation for the Cambridge Higher Local, and for the examinations of London University, including those for the degrees of M.A., B.A., B.Sc. This section of its work entitles Cheltenham to a place among the colleges devoted to higher or university education.

The third school visited was one of the Girls' Public Day Schools Company at Notting Hill, under Miss **A Girls' Public Day School.** Jones. This was the second school opened by the Company in September, 1873, the first having been at Chelsea, in January. Notting Hill began with ten pupils; for many years it has had its complement, 400. The school was rebuilt in 1883, and has now a hall and series of pleasant class-rooms. It is, however, by no means the best or newest building the Company has erected. Among the compulsory subjects are mathematics, French, German, Latin. Each language is begun in a different year; moreover, Greek is frequently taken in the upper forms, since it is compulsory for certain examinations. All classes take a science subject, such as botany, physiology, chemistry; there is a special science teacher directing this work. Drawing is compulsory as far as the upper fifth form. Sewing and physical exercises have each a weekly lesson. The proportion of pupils is twenty-two to each teacher. A fair proportion of the students pass on to college life; others enter the Post Office, Savings Banks, and employments open to women. Work is tested by the examination of the Joint Board, and the whole school examined annually by an examiner of the Oxford and Cambridge Schools Examination Board.

The two schools first described are unique, the lifework of two pioneers in women's education. The **The Skinners' Co.'s Middle School for Girls, Stamford Hill, London, N.** Skinners' School, at Stamford Hill, is on another footing, one of a type of schools happily becoming more common. The Skinners' Company had already built three schools for boys, when it was suggested to them, presumably, that there exist such beings as girls. Having funds at their disposal, they fell in with the idea that their next school should be for them. The foundations were laid, and the school opened in 1890. The Charity Commissioners provided a scheme, and the whole work was so welcomed by the neighbourhood and proved so highly successful, that in 1893 the original building, intended to accommodate 200, had to be enlarged to hold 350. The Company had gained the services of an able head-mistress, Miss Page, who had up till then been head of a school under the Girls' Public Day School Company. The Skinners' School is second grade, girls remaining up to sixteen or seventeen years of age, and working to the standard of the lower and, when possible, the higher examinations of the Joint Board of Oxford and Cambridge. The curriculum of this school having been made liberal by the scheme of the Charity Commissioners, the standard of work is the same as in the middle and lower parts of those high schools where girls remain up to nineteen years of age. The Great Hall is an admirable room, light and beautiful, with a raised platform, capable of adaptation to many purposes. Behind it is a memorial window, with memorials of Thomas Hunt and Lawrence Atwell, at which one gazes reverently. Light and airy class-rooms, beautifully furnished, open off the sides of the hall. The playground is good, judged by the London standard. Nothing could be better than the arrangement of the cloak-rooms: the seat underneath the girl's peg; the wires below the seat on which to place boots; the shelf above the peg for books whilst their owner is dressing, all convince the visitor that some one who has studied girls' needs had planned them. A gymnasium, a studio, laboratory, and dining-room deserve to be mentioned. The fees are low, from £4 to £10, and this is perhaps the reason why the classes average thirty or forty in number. Indeed, the classes in all the girls' public schools visited by the writer are far too large, even when the fees are much higher than at the Skinners' School. The curriculum embraces the usual subjects, with a good deal of option and consideration for individual ability. Drawing is compulsory up to the sixth form; sewing up to the fifth. A fair amount of science teaching is carried on in this school, and the science mistress commented upon the interest shewn in it. The girls seemed to be of much the same class as in a school of the G.P.D.S. Company; but with a larger percentage of those whose parents are not wealthy. Similar schools are the Aske's School, at Hatcham; the Haberdashers' School, at Hoxton; Dame Alice Owen's School, Islington; and the James Allen School, at Dulwich.

It would be well if some of our provincial teachers, working in comparatively dismal surroundings, could see the admirable new buildings that are now springing up, especially when the children are at work in them. Light, airy, and often charmingly decorated, they favourably affect the character of the teaching, and the temperament of the taught.

SECTION III.

฿igber Ebucation

[I.]

HIGHER education is here assumed to mean education in colleges connected with the universities, or in **Definition.** colleges of university rank, carried on after the age of eighteen or thereabouts. It must be noted that in Britain there are a number of excellent secondary schools where an upper class or classes receive a considerable part of a collegiate education.

It is necessary to guard against the error that higher education for women is peculiar to the nineteenth **Higher Education not a Novelty.** century. This proceeds from a survey confined to the seventeenth, eighteenth, and early nineteenth centuries; if we turn to the work of women in the monasteries, we recognize that woman's share in education varies at different epochs. Miss Eckenstein shows, in *Woman under Monasticism*, how women shared the culture of their day, especially during the early days of monasticism, the sixth to the eighth centuries, and in its golden age, the twelfth. In the first period we find abbesses taking part in politics, affixing their signature to documents in token of dignity and assurance of royal good faith ; Hilda of Whitby ruled over a monastery of men and women ; five of the men who studied under her were raised to the episcopate.

As poets, letter-writers, translators, transcribers, artists, nuns took a respectable place. In the tenth century, **Literary and** Hrotswith wrote dramatic plays in **Artistic activity** Latin at Gandersheim ; Ebert tells of **of Nuns.** her fruitful poetic talent, and how in Latin drama she stands alone ; in the twelfth century, Herrad produces at Hohenburg, in Alsace, her *Garden of Delights*, an account of the history of the world illustrated with pictures probably drawn by herself and coloured by the nuns. Two of these pictures caused Gérard to classify Herrad as among the most imaginative painters the world has known. Gradually the nuns gave up such work for devotion ; their whole time became absorbed in ritual ; their life divorced from practical affairs. Reformers industriously preached that there was no career for woman apart from wifehood and motherhood. Henry VIII. permitted Cromwell, Layton, and Legh to annex or destroy the nunneries, driving forth all those—the great majority—who were unwilling to go, and giving their buildings, lands, revenues to others, sometimes for the endowment of men's colleges.* It should be recollected that the

* The nunnery of St. Radegund was transformed into Jesus College, Cambridge, by the good offices of the Bishop of Ely ; Fisher, Bishop of Rochester, used his interest to hand over

women who were founding colleges and professorships for men, as did Margaret Beaufort, shared the view that women's education was of no importance, and swelled **Growing indiffer-** the growing indifference to the in- **ence to Women's** tellectual attainments of their sex. **intellectual life.** Practically the Reformation reclaimed even the unmarried woman for the home, but remained indifferent to the culture and intelligence with which she is now expected to dignify it.   This curious belittling of the home ideal still secures the practical adhesion of considerable numbers, and affords a striking instance of misplaced humility.

Enough has been written to prove that the higher education of women is not entirely a new movement, but rather a revival.

There have been always those who directed sneers and satires against women's ignorance : especially was **Ridicule poured** this the case in the eighteenth century. **on learned** During the early years of the eighteenth **Women.** century, we find Mary Astell, in Chelsea, urging better education for women.   She was followed by Mary Wollstonecraft, in her *Rights of Woman.*   In

Bromhall Nunnery and Lillchurch to St. John's College, Cambridge ; Wolsey gave St. Frideswith's to Cardinal College, Oxford, now known as Christ Church, and possessing the largest income from endowment of all the Oxford colleges.   Some of the prioresses opposed this wholesale confiscation ; but it was no easy task to withstand Henry VIII. and his minions.   If the prioress would not yield, and sign papers transferring the nunnery to the King, she was deposed for a more pliant head.   See Miss ECKENSTEIN's chapter on "The Dissolution in England."

the beginning of the present century Sydney Smith rebuked the accomplishment craze which would seek to embellish a few years of woman's life, "years which are in themselves so full of grace and happiness, that they hardly want it, and then leaves the rest of existence a prey to idle insignificance." Jean Paul Richter, whose father and grandfather before him were teachers, rebuked parents who sin against their daughters by "shewing or recommending, even indirectly, any excellence they may possess—be it art, science, or the sanctuary of the heart—as a lure to men, or a bait for catching a husband." In our own day, Mr. James Bryce alludes to the fact "that women have minds as cultivable, and as well worth cultivating, as men's minds, is still regarded by the ordinary British parent as an offensive, not to say a revolutionary paradox." Whatever respect social conventions have accorded to the ignorant woman in society, occasionally she has been told the plain truth.

We should naturally expect to find that the movement for the higher education of women during the present **Beginnings of the Modern Movement in Education.** century has its origin in more causes than one. About 1833 the Birkbeck Literary and Scientific Institution opened its classes to women, acknowledging their claims before they had begun to urge them. On inquiry, the Principal, Mr. G. Armitage-Smith, reports that women were first admitted to single lectures delivered twice a week in the theatre on educational and scientific subjects. Later these lectures developed into full courses given in class-rooms. At a date subsequent to 1833, a formal resolution was passed admitting women to the full advantages of the Institution. The present Secrerary reports that the date of this resolution was long before that of his appointment (1851). As far as can now be learned, there was no agitation, nor even special applications by women. A storm of ridicule from a certain section of the press is said to have greeted this action of the Council, but the Institution has never turned back on this policy. In her able article upon "University Education for Women in England,"* Mrs. Henry Fawcett shews how women's first, formal, organized claim to the rights of citizenship dates from 1840, when two American ladies, Mrs. Mott and Mrs. Stanton, were excluded, on the ground of sex, from an anti-slavery convention held in London, to which they had been sent as delegates. The two movements for education and citizenship are of course closely united.

In 1841 we find the Governesses' Benevolent Institution beginning to move. It was formally organized in

Governesses' 1843; it aimed at the assistance of
Benevolent governesses in temporary difficulties,
Institution. annuities for them, a home for the
aged, and free registration. Soon we find the Committee (presumably men) and the Ladies' Committee face to face with want of qualification and competency. There must be a diploma; the governesses must themselves be taught. The Report of 1846 expressly tells

* Addresses and Proceedings of International Congress of Education, Chicago, 1893.

us that "the Committee were not prepared to find the higher authorities of the country unawakened to the importance of female education, in its bearing upon national character, and thus upon national prosperity," and there are seditious allusions to the monopoly of endowments and universities by the privileged sex. This report was the work of the Rev. David Laing, then honorary secretary, a consistent advocate of women's education. The Report for 1847 tells of arrangements being made to commence classes in all departments of education, and of the gentlemen who formed the Education Committee of the Governesses' Benevolent Institution busy examining the governesses, and giving them certificates.

Next year Queen's College opened in Harley Street, for "an improved system of female education with

Opening of Queen's College, 1848. such prospects and such success as its most sanguine friends dared not anticipate." The first term there were 200 entries, and 45 lectures given per week by such men as the Rev. F. D. Maurice, Dean Plumptre, R. C. Trench (afterwards Archbishop of Dublin), Dr. Brewer, and others. The college was really a branch of the Institution ; governesses who were members had the right of attending certain lectures free.* In 1853 it

* They sent this letter of thanks to the Committee in 1849 :

"The ladies who have enjoyed the privilege of attending the Evening Classes, are anxious to express their gratitude to those gentlemen who have so kindly contributed to their improvement, and who have devoted so much time to that purpose.

"They are deeply sensible of the great benefit which they have separated from its parent, and began an independent career with a Royal Charter of Incorporation; ladies of rank and title became visitors to the college, among them Lady Stanley of Alderley.   As the instruction at Queen's College was given in accordance with the principles of the Church of England, that large body of educated opinion which has always objected to religious tests helped to found another college for women in Bedford Square, on an undenominational basis, in 1849.   To this end Mrs. John Reid lent solid help.

Amongst the early scholars of Queen's College we find Miss Buss and Miss Beale; at Bedford College were George Eliot, Mrs. Craik, Anna Swanwick, Mme. Bodichon, while Miss Clough and Miss Emily Davies sat on the Committee.

The movement for the higher education of women received help also from the College of Preceptors, founded in 1846.   It is true that at first the College was intended for men only, but soon a Ladies' Department arises, under the auspices of Miss Edgeworth, Miss M. A. Strickland, and other able women.   Happily this was allowed to drop, and in 1849 women were admitted to the College, profiting by much of its educational programme.   By 1850 we

The College of Preceptors— Women admitted, 1849.

derived from the various Lectures; and unanimously feel that they cannot suffer the Term to close without offering their sincere thanks to all the Professors for their valuable instructions."

About forty signatures were attached.

may say that the higher education movement was safely launched.

The position of Bedford is unique among the women's colleges. Its history covers the whole period of the Revival of Learning among women.

Bedford College, 1849.
It is not only a hall of residence for about 40 out of 200 students, it supplies all the teaching necessary for the examinations of London University. Moreover, it must shortly be recognized as a constituent college of London University, and is now subsidized by Parliament; it also receives a handsome donation from the London County Council for technical instruction.

The state of Secondary Education was so poor during the early life of Bedford College, that for 15 years the Council managed a secondary school, only giving it up in 1868 to devote itself entirely to higher education. In 1874 the College removed to Baker Street, where it has extended itself backward to East Street. It now possesses six excellent laboratories, erected at a cost of more than £6000.

Bedford does not aim at the exact assimilation of a curriculum for women to one for men. Provision was made in 1895 for instruction in art, and music is duly recognized. Bedford College is much indebted to its able and vigorous Council. When the Parliamentary

Share in the Parliamentary Grant.
Grant of £15,000 per annum was first divided among university colleges, Bedford was passed over. Some of the Council worked hard to obtain a share of this

K

money, and gained it in 1894, when the grants were revised. The Council are sometimes accused of appointing men to vacant professorships ; but their defence is that they always choose the ablest teacher, regardless of sex distinction. A large proportion of Bedford students work for the examinations of London University.

The fate of Queen's College has been different. The Schools Inquiry Commission observed, in 1868, in its report, that it has almost entirely taken up secondary education. It now has a middle school for girls up to the age of fourteen, and courses in the College proper for students between about fourteen and eighteen, the course covering four years.

About the sixties, educational associations of women arose in different parts of the country. At Liverpool **Educational** we find a Ladies' Educational Society **Associations of** in 1866, which led to the University **Women.** Extension movement ; at Leeds, the Yorkshire Ladies' Council of Education ; in London, 1871, the National Union for Improving the Education of Women.

Whilst the Schools Inquiry Commission was sitting in 1865–67, Miss Emily Davies presented a memorial **A famous** to the members, signed by twelve **Memorial.** notable women, chiefly teachers, drawing attention to the great need that existed of a place of education for adult female students, and alluding to such a foundation as amongst the most urgent educational wants of the time. The memorial was endorsed by the signatures of nearly

200 persons, amongst them Kay-Shuttleworth, Huxley, Ruskin, Canon Norris, Lyell, Paget, Tennyson, Browning, Grote, Tyndall, Grant Duff, Stansfeld, Bain, R. C. Jebb, Lyulph Stanley, J. E. Gorst. About 25 of the signatures are women's, the remainder belonging to professors, scientists, men distinguished in literature, art, and politics. Of course nothing, not even the signatures of this memorial, can convince minds of a certain order that the movement for the higher education of women is anything but a blow aimed at the supremacy of one sex.

This bold idea of a college for women, connected with one of the ancient universities, owes its inception to Miss Emily Davies, first presenting itself to her mind as a practical project in October, 1866. It commended itself to the London Schoolmistresses' Association, who throughout lent cordial assistance. The memorial already alluded to was presented on July 9th, 1867, and for the next two years we find Miss Davies and her friends busy collecting £3000 to found the new college. A house was taken at Hitchin, in 1869, and work began with six students; this was

Girton College, 1869.

the modest beginning of Girton College. It excited a fair amount of ridicule, disapproval,* and more or less good-humoured banter.

---

* "There is no doubt that this sort of woman," says a *Quarterly Reviewer* in 1869, "will not be popular with men." Probably he had not seen the memorial just alluded to. He goes on to say that this new college might have his approval if the students were taught to sew, teach, keep house, read aloud, make their own dresses, and be helpful at mission working parties.

In 1873 the young college removed to Girton, two miles from Cambridge, where, by a series of extensions, accommodation now exists for 104 students, exclusive of the teaching staff and officials. The buildings are excellent; every year the grounds become more beautiful, but the distance from Cambridge is, in some respects, disadvantageous. It is an open secret that the executive deferred to public opinion in planting the women students so far from the town; they could not possibly foresee that public opinion would rapidly veer round to their side, and leave them in the position of having over-estimated their opponents' sense of propriety.

The women's colleges are so carefully managed and financed that the average of comfort, of a pleasant, and even enjoyable, existence, is high. Women co-operate more than is the case in men's colleges, almost all meals being taken in hall. One result is that the cost of their maintenance is usually smaller.

By its memorandum of association Girton College must provide for the students' instruction and for religious services in accordance with the principles of the Church of England; a conscience clause prevents friction. Since the foundation, 575 students have been in residence, and of these the large number of 370 have obtained honours according to the Cambridge University standard, and hold the "equivalent of a degree." The College has rigorously maintained that the students' work must be judged by the standards recognized by the university. Few will doubt that this was a wise policy to begin with. Up to 1881, when formal permission was given to women to sit for the

Formal permission for Women to sit for the Degree Examination, 1881. degree examination, students who did not read for honours at Girton used to read for the ordinary degree; but this has been given up since 1882. Formal permission to sit for the University Honours Examinations marks a great step in advance. It was partly due to the success of Miss Charlotte Scott, who in 1880 took the mathematical tripos, and was bracketed with the eighth wrangler. This aroused extraordinary enthusiasm both among men and women. In 1887 the only person at Cambridge who attained the first division of the first class in the classical tripos was Miss A. F. Ramsay. In one year Girton had seven first classes: the college is small, and it was pointed out at the time that if a large men's college had obtained as many, it would have done admirably. But, indeed, successes at the women's colleges are now far too common to excite much attention save in academic circles and in the women's papers.

Newnham was founded in consequence of a demand by women at a distance to share the advantages of

Newnham College, 1871. certain lectures given specially to women by Cambridge University men. In 1871 Miss A. J. Clough took a house in Cambridge for five students. Year by year the college has steadily developed until it now includes three halls—Clough, Sidgwick, and Old Hall, and stands on a site of more than eight acres. It accommodates 158 students, besides the teaching staff and other officials. Past and present students now number 1050; of these, 433 have passed in the various triposes, mathematics, classics, moral sciences, natural sciences, history, mediæval and modern languages, law. Tripos examinations are, of course, those through which men obtain honour degrees. Newnham is entirely unsectarian, no religious test having ever been imposed. Fees payable to the college amount to 75 guineas per annum. Students have mainly bed‑sitting‑rooms at Newnham, whereas at Girton they enjoy the luxury of two rooms, and pay fees amounting to 100 guineas.

Newnham, too, has her notable successes: in 1890 Miss Philippa Fawcett was placed above the Senior Wrangler. In 1891 she was also in the first division of the first class in part II. of the mathematical tripos. In 1893 Miss A. M. Johnson was placed between the fifth and sixth wranglers. Next year she was the only person in the first division of the first class in part II. of the tripos. In 1895, out of 49 students who entered for tripos examinations from Newnham, 12 took first classes, 24 second classes, 12 third classes, and one an aegrotat.

The position of women at Cambridge is peculiar. They are students; Girton and Newnham are recog‑

Position of Women at Cambridge. nized as hostels, residence at which for a certain length of time, together with the passing of preliminary ex‑ aminations prescribed by the University, confers the

right of entering for examination for honour degrees.
A man is legally a member of the University even
during his undergraduateship. Neither as undergraduate, nor as holder of the equivalent of a degree,
is a woman a member of the University. She may not
enter for the ordinary degree examination, only for
honour degrees. In 1880 a great attempt was made
to open Cambridge degrees to women. It was unsuccessful; but resulted in formal permission for women
to enter for the honour examinations. In 1887 the
agitation was renewed with no result whatever, the
University refusing even to consider the question. It
was opened up again in 1896. The Council of the
Senate then appointed a syndicate to consider what
further privileges (if any) should be granted to women
in Cambridge, and whether they should be admitted to
degrees. The Syndicate has been instructed to report
before the end of Michaelmas term, 1896, and the
agitators are not without hope that some concession
may be made, though it is doubtful whether they will
obtain the just treatment which London has afforded
to women.

The women's colleges—and this remark applies to
them all—have greatly helped to raise the status of the
The Colleges teaching profession, which a large
and the Teaching proportion of their students enter.
Profession. Miss Kennedy, when collecting information in 1894 about the occupations of former
Newnham students, found that out of a total of 720,
374 entered women's great profession. Other students

become doctors, journalists, bookbinders, gardeners, clerks to the Labour Commission, secretaries, missionaries; 230 returned to live at home, and of these 108 married. Miss Constance Jones is of opinion that about two-thirds of the Girton students become teachers; but no precise calculation has yet been made.

At Oxford the position of women is not so satisfactory as at Cambridge, inasmuch as the University does not grant certificates to women who pass honour examinations, in the same way as Cambridge grants them to those who have passed triposes. (These certificates are given to women only, never to men.) At Oxford, women's colleges are smaller and more numerous than at Cambridge. There are now four, since St. Hilda's, a house established as a branch for students connected with the Ladies' College at Cheltenham, has quite recently taken rank as a hall. It may here be noted that the examinations at Oxford were formally opened to women in 1884.

Women at Oxford.

Somerville Hall and Lady Margaret Hall both started in 1879, each with nine students. The stated objects of the founders of Somerville are "to afford young women, at moderate expense, such facilities for their higher education as will enable them better to fulfil the duties of life, and, if need be, to earn an honourable and independent livelihood, and to help forward the education of women throughout the country." Somerville

Somerville Hall, 1879.

has twice been enlarged, and now affords accommodation for seventy students. Up to June, 1896, 225 students had been in residence, of whom 120 had passed an honour examination similar to that taken by men as the degree course. Somerville is named after Mary Somerville ; it is the largest of the three halls, and is the only undenominational hall for women at Oxford. Miss Maitland is the Principal.

Lady Margaret Hall is named after Lady Margaret Tudor, mother of Henry VII. It has added house to house during its existence, and can now accommodate forty-eight students. In October, 1896, it removed to new buildings close to the old hall. Since opening, 210 students have passed through Lady Margaret, many of whom are now teachers. The Secretary reports that all but a very few lectures are now open to women students at Oxford.

Lady Margaret Hall, 1879.

St. Hugh's was begun by Miss Wordsworth, the Principal of Lady Margaret, for the education of twenty-five students who could not afford the fees of Lady Margaret Hall. This college is named after St. Hugh of Lincoln. There are also home students residing in Oxford, not members of any hall. Altogether, the women's colleges at Oxford accommodate about 150 students. The conditions and regulations that obtain there are not readily comprehended, and require a word of explanation.

St. Hugh's Hall, 1886.

Women are not required to reside in a "hostel";

they may live in their own houses at Oxford, or not

in Oxford at all. Even for men, residence is only required for the degree. Women have also been permitted to enter for final examinations without taking the whole course required for the degree, though, as a matter of fact, the class obtained in an honour examination of the University is clearly indicated on the certificate received, and such certificate is of more importance than minor examinations that may or may not have been omitted. Hence there has arisen a good deal of uncertainty as to the value and significance of the Oxford certificates. To remedy this uncertainty, an Association for the Education of Women at Oxford has been founded. It provides lectures, arranges private tuition, and, above all, issues two diplomas, one granted only to students who have taken the full degree course with honours, and resided the requisite three years, and another granted to those who have taken an alternative course of three examinations approved by the Council, and who have resided the same length of time. The value of the Oxford student's course will thus be apparent to anyone who understands the University curriculum. A certificate will be given to resident students who have taken an honour examination but have not qualified for the diploma.

The proposal to admit women to the B.A. degree at Oxford was brought before the Congregation of the University in March, 1896, by means of the Association for the Education of Women at Oxford, and rejected by 215 votes to 140. Great efforts were made on both sides, and it will hardly be possible to agitate again for some years.

Perhaps few things are more conspicuous, in making a tour of the women's colleges, than the devotion of **Pious Founders.** the students, and indeed of all concerned in the management, to the pious founder. They have no monopoly of this attitude of mind : but whereas William of Wyckham, Margaret Beaufort, Wolsey, and the rest of the noble army of founders, are somewhat remote from modern life, the movement for women's education is still so young that the pious woman founder has been personally known, her life felt as a living influence. As an illustration, Newnham set up, in 1894, beautiful bronze gates as a memorial to Miss Clough. "She would have cared little that her name should be lost, if her work went on," observed one of the speakers at the opening ceremony. The students, and above all the older women who sit on college councils, and who were often deprived in youth of the opportunities of a fuller and freer life which women now enjoy, are determined that names like hers shall not be lost. When new wings, halls, laboratories, libraries are opened, or scholarships founded, the names of Reid, Clough, Pfeiffer, Kennedy, Bodichon, Sidgwick, Stanley of Alderley, are commemorated with great enthusiasm. The business energy of these pioneers, the courage with which they faced ridicule, the tact with which they disarmed opposition and rallied to their side waverers as well as conscientious adherents of both sexes, the devotion shewn in giving or collecting money to extend or free from debt women's institutions, could not indeed well be forgotten.

The University of London was the first academic body in the United Kingdom to throw open its degrees, **Women** honours, prizes to students of both **in London** sexes, on terms of perfect equality. **University.** This it did in 1878, by means of a supplemental charter. Previously the University had attempted to meet the demand for the improved education of women by instituting special examinations for them. But those for whom they were intended thought little of the privilege conferred, shewed no wish for exclusive instruction, and it soon became evident that women must have the same tests or qualifications as men. Doubtless it was in the women's favour that London is not a teaching university, and that its charter dates from 1836. No conditions of residence having been laid down, and no accretions of past centuries having to be broken through, the opening of the said degrees, honours, and prizes has been a far easier task than that which Oxford and Cambridge must presently face. The women's charter of 1878 was itself a result of the wide educational movement which has been faintly traced; but it has also become the cause of further developments, and, despite a growing feeling among educationists that examination has a cramping as well as a hurrying effect upon development, and that too large a proportion regard examination as an end in itself, has encouraged and inspired a movement growing in depth and volume.

Successes at London University. The following is a list of women's successes in the examinations of London University, completed to Dec. 1895. Where a degree is conferred by such success, the letters follow :—

ARTS.

Matriculation . . .	3762	
Intermediate Arts . . .	991	
Bachelor of Arts . . .	603	B.A.
Master of Arts . . .	49	M.A.
Doctor of Literature . .	1	D.Lit.
Intermediate Science . .	181	
Bachelor of Science . .	106	B.Sc.
Doctor of Science . . .	5	D.Sc.

MEDICINE.

Preliminary Scientific . .	167	
Intermediate Medicine . .	73	
Bachelor of Medicine . .	53	M.B.
Doctor of Medicine . .	15	M.D.
Bachelor of Surgery . .	10	B.S.
Master of Surgery . .	1	M.S.

During the sixty years that London University has been an examining body only, much of its teaching **University College, London.** has been obtainable at University College, and King's College, Strand. The classes at the former are conducted by able professors, and with one notable exception—that of medicine—are alike open to men and women. There is no separate department for women; they attend the professors' classes along with men, "sitting cheek by jowl," as opponents of co-education phrase it. A lady superintendent (Miss Morison) has a certain oversight of all women students; and for those for whom residence is desired, it can be found at College Hall, Byng Place, under the care of Miss Grove. As an experiment in co-education, there can be little doubt that the system used at University College has been perfectly successful. If the size of a class compels a professor to divide it, surely few practical teachers will deny that ability rather than sex should usually form the line of division. In all, about 400 women attend the classes at University College. Of these, a majority are working for degrees; but a certain number follow classes in fine art, Egyptology, archæology, and similar subjects. Thirty-four students find residence at College Hall. With regard to the position of women as members of London University, it is satisfactory to note that, as graduates, women are duly qualified members. The Charter of 1878 enacted that no woman should be a member of Convocation until a resolution should be passed to that effect. This was done on January 17th, 1882, practically as soon as women were qualified; and now they vote, and take part in all the proceedings of Convocation, shewing great interest.

The ladies' classes connected with King's College

seem to partake largely of the nature of the University
Extension movement, and adapt themselves a good
King's College, deal to the requirements of a wealthy
Ladies' London suburb. The Ladies' Depart-
Department. ment is situated in Kensington Square.
Lectures are given by the professors of King's College,
or other lecturers appointed from time to time to
lecture on a subject for which a special desire has
been expressed, *e.g.* Wagner, Browning. There is
no residence attached; and though a certain number
of students prepare for university examinations, the
majority are ladies living at home, desirous of
working up certain subjects in which they feel an
interest. Such students number between 300 and 400,
and if they pass in a sufficient number of subjects, and
remain two years at the College, receive a diploma.
Weekly paper work and a terminal examination are
features of the work. The subjects taken are very
various, embracing ancient and modern history,
literature, languages, ethics, art, music, mathematics,
domestic economy, recitation, wood-carving, and so
forth. It is proposed to begin a class of students
who shall work for the arts examinations of London
University.

Two colleges specially for women remain to be
mentioned. Westfield College is an outcome of the
Westfield resolution taken by the University of
College, 1882. London, in 1878, to open its degrees,
honours, and prizes to women on the
same footing as they are open to men. Places of study

to obtain the degrees of a non-resident university became necessary; they therefore arose. Westfield was founded in 1882 with the avowed object of preparing women for London degrees, and affording them residence. The trust deeds declare that there shall be in the College religious teaching of a strictly Protestant character, "in conformity with the principles of the Reformation and in harmony with the doctrines of the Church of England," though students need not necessarily be members of that Church. The mistress, Miss E. L. Maynard, one of the earliest students at Girton, is under the control of a Council. At first the College carried on its work in private houses at Hampstead; it was so successful that in 1891 a large wing was built facing the south-east. There is room for 45 students, whose zeal, and the ability of the teachers, cause no small share of the degrees, honours, and prizes of London University to fall to the College. As is usual with women's colleges, Westfield is hampered by want of funds and scholarships; it possesses several laboratories, but for physics is obliged to send its students to work at Bedford College, whose laboratories are probably the best for women in the kingdom. Westfield, whose existence is largely due to the munificence of Miss Dudin Browne, stands in three acres of its own grounds, and provides each student comfortably with sitting and bed-room. The fees are £105 per annum, with no extras; the college even pays examination fees.

People who have never taken the short journey from

Waterloo to Egham, some twenty-one miles, will probably be as surprised as the writer to
find the College built upon a scale
of unparalleled magnificence, and with
an extraordinary completeness of service arrangement.
What strikes one at the first glance is the unity of
design ; the College is what architects term the result
of one act of conception, the successive stages of a
single intellectual effort. The style is French Renais-
sance. Those who are acquainted with the Château de
Chambord tell us that though it is built of white stone,
whereas the College is of red brick faced with Portland
stone, the general effect of the two structures is not
dissimilar. Holloway College covers more ground
than any other women's college in the world ; it forms
a double quadrangle, measuring 550 feet by 375 feet.
The two long blocks are each five stories high, and
are mainly used for the housing of students, each having
her own sitting and bed-room. The buildings which
connect these two great blocks, the corridors of which
are a tenth of a mile long, embrace a chapel to the left
of the vestibule on entering, highly ornate, and with
barrel roof ; on the right, a picture gallery containing
an excellent collection of modern paintings ; the central
connecting block contains on one side the handsome
dining hall, on the other the kitchens ; the last connecting
block contains a library and museum, both beautifully
fitted, though the furnishing of the latter is scarcely
begun. The library is subsidized to the extent of
£200 per annum, of which £150 purchases new books,

Royal Holloway College, 1887.

L

There are besides a sanatorium in the grounds, chemical and biological laboratories, an excellent swimming bath, a gymnasium fitted up with every possible requisite, a clock tower, water tower, an installation of electric light, twelve music - rooms with deadened walls, a racquet court. The whole building stands in ninety-six acres of ground, including, of course, cricket pitch and tennis courts. It is said that the College was built to accommodate 250 students, with ample room for the staff and servants; the total number of rooms is about eight hundred. The founder, Mr. Thomas Holloway, who died in 1883, built the College by the advice and counsel of his wife, and spent upon it the princely sum of £800,000; the building alone cost £257,000.

It was in the founder's mind that this great and imposing building should form the nucleus of a women's university, in course of time conferring its own degrees on students. The dead hand of the past was not to rest heavily upon it, Mr. Holloway holding the belief that women's education should not be exclusively regulated by the traditions and methods of former ages. No doubt he showed wisdom in giving prominence to drawing and painting in the curriculum as well as music; certain service rooms could easily be used for practical instruction in cookery what time women choose to release themselves from the bondage of examination curricula laid down by men for men. Already courses of instruction have been given in cookery, ambulance work, sick nursing, wood carving, dressmaking. Meantime Holloway has only some ninety students, who mostly prepare for the examinations of London University and of Oxford. At the time of writing (July, 1896), some sixty students of Holloway have graduated in the University of London in arts and science. The laboratories of the College include some thirteen or fourteen rooms, fitted up with everything that a student in natural science could possibly need. Candidates for admission must be over seventeen; the fees are £90 per annum, with very few extras.

The College was opened in October, 1887, and has already gained very considerable university distinctions. Perhaps one of its least admirable features is the smallness and insignificance of the lecture theatre, quite a low room in the basement. Doubtless, should the numbers grow, the handsome hall now known as the museum could be utilized for lecturing purposes. The friends of women's education will probably closely watch the development of Holloway College for one reason, if for no other. By the will of the founder, men only are its trustees and governors. It is a trite observation that where women's colleges and educational institutions have taken firm root, where their progress has been rapid, and at the same time solid, both initiation and management have been largely in the hands of women themselves. Men have helped ungrudgingly, but only helped. A comparison between England and Germany is here worth making. The direction of women's education in England lies mainly in the hands of women; in Germany this is not the case, and it is but too well known that a vivifying influence makes its lack plentifully felt. The German system seems something laid on women instead of springing from their own initiative, warmed by their own energy. Of course, this question has no relation to the need and desirability of mixed staffs, which are used in all the university colleges, or colleges of university rank, for women, both in England and Wales. In somes cases the staff itself is not mixed; but the fact that students attend the classes of famous lecturers causes the difference to be mainly one of words.

Share of Women in University Colleges

The Victoria University has three constituent colleges: Owens, Manchester, founded in 1851; Yorkshire College, Leeds, 1874; and Liverpool College, 1881. The University grants degrees; each college makes it own regulations and teaching arrangements. There are now 674 men and 89 women graduates of Victoria University; 81 are graduates in arts, 6 in science, 2 in music. The women attend convocation on exactly the same conditions as men. They are practically excluded from the medical faculty, which adversely affects their numbers. No woman has yet attempted to take a degree in law.

Victoria University, 1880.

The attitude of Owens to women students in the past can hardly be styled cordial. It was expressly founded to instruct and improve "young persons of the male

Owens College, 1851.

sex." Even in 1871, when it obtained the power to open the College classes to women, it carefully protected the young male person by its famous clause: "conditionally upon adequate provision having been made for the instruction of male applicants." It has never opened its medical department to women, though law and engineering are permitted to receive them. Numbers of the Owens scholarships are for men only. The numbers of men students are 1196, as compared with 108 women. Nowhere else can be remarked so striking a disparity in the proportions of the sexes, and it is difficult to account for, unless the attitude of Owens towards women in past days is a sufficient explanation.

The Registrar of Victoria University states that at one time Manchester women went to Liverpool College for science teaching. Another authority observes that only one did so; but even if this be so, a single unit cannot represent the amount of repression and discouragement which women must have suffered.

A women's department has, however, grown up, and in course of time even Owens has gone back on its exclusive policy. All but the medical classes are now open. Owens has shewn readiness to adopt the University Extension system, and arranges for courses of lectures to both sexes in the neighbourhood of Manchester.

The Yorkshire College, Leeds, in its memorandum of association undertakes to promote the education of both

Yorkshire College, Leeds, 1874. sexes. It is partly an outcome of the University Extension movement, and of the need for technical instruction at an important manufacturing centre. It amalgamated with the Leeds School of Medicine in 1884. Women are admitted to this school, but not allowed to attend the Leeds Infirmary for clinical instruction, an essential part of the course for qualification, so that practically the medical faculty is closed to women. There is no separate department for women; both sexes attend the same classes. The total number of students, 1896, is, men, 840; women, 143.

Liverpool College co-operates in the University Extension movement. The College was opened in 1882 for **Liverpool College, incorporated 1881.** the instruction of the "residents of Liverpool," amongst whom the women are included. They enjoy equally with men the privileges of the College, attending the same lectures and classes, with the exception that the School of Medicine is closed to them. The average attendance for each of the three terms is 332, of whom 73 are women. Liverpool College is unfortunately burdened with a rather heavy debt, despite its Government grant of £1533 per annum. The Council are averse from effecting economies which would impair efficiency.

The University of Wales is composed of three constituent colleges, formed into the University of Wales **University of Wales, 1893.** in 1893. The colleges are Aberystwyth, founded in 1872; Cardiff, in 1883; and Bangor, in 1884. Each college receives a Government subvention of £4000 per annum. Before the University of Wales received power to confer its own degrees, the students in Welsh colleges worked successfully for the degrees of London and other universities. The colleges possess equal rights and privileges ; but as Aberystwyth is a dozen years older than the others, it may fairly be regarded as both pioneer and premier college. Men and women are on an absolute equality as regards degrees, entrance to classes, and, what is equally important, social life. The governing body have, moreover, tried the experiment of mixed education ; men and women, staff and students alike, meet in class-rooms, share in debates, entertainments, concerts, with excellent results. The fees have been made as low as possible, and it is probably owing to this fact that the numbers of the sexes tend to approximate. In October, 1896, there were 222 men and 153 women students. A hall of residence, Alexandra Hall, capable of accommodating 150 women, was opened by the Princess of Wales in July, 1896; and a wing to accommodate another fifty students is in contemplation. Residence in hall is practically compulsory for the women students. The College has a strong technical side : classes are conducted in scientific agriculture, dairy farming, cookery, and so forth. The Council have thus recognized the needs of the country, and adapted the College to them. The thorough education afforded, the equality on which the sexes are placed, the excellence of the management under Miss E. A. Carpenter, the low fees, are attracting considerable numbers of Englishwomen. In the Lent term of 1884 there was one woman student at Aberystwyth; now there are 153.

At Cardiff, an important engineering department, women reside at Aberdare Hall, and are admitted to the Medical School. Bangor, which has an agricultural department, has also a hostel for women. The course for the degrees of the University of Wales covers three years; the first matriculation examination was held in 1895.

Durham University was founded in 1831, and consists of (a) a theological school at Durham, (b) a college of medicine, founded in 1851 and in-

Durham University.

corporated with the University 1852, and (c) a college of science at Newcastle, 1871.

In 1883 arose the question of granting degrees to women, when Convocation unanimously resolved to confer them. The growth of the Newcastle colleges in the new buildings erected in 1887 and 1888, the applications for the admission of women to the College of Medicine, made the matter one of considerable importance. In June, 1893, Miss Ella Bryant, who had passed all the examinations for the B.Sc. degree of the University, tendered her fee for the degree. It was refused until a supplementary charter could be obtained. The new charter was applied for almost immediately afterwards, and granted in 1895. The opening of another university to women excited hardly any attention either at the time or afterwards, and marks the growth of the sentiment that if anything is closed to women, it is natural that it should be opened. The opening of the degrees does not extend to theology, as, for some occult reason, the British people regard divinity as a purely masculine pursuit. In 1892 a vicar of the Church of England at Folkestone proposed to withdraw from various committees of the Church Congress because a lady was announced to address it. Only the fatherly guidance of the Bishop of Dover prevented him carrying out this threat.

It may fairly be said that the opening of these degrees is due to the growth and flourishing condition of the Newcastle colleges. The numbers, July 1896, are as follows :—

	Men.	Women.
College of Medicine ...	220 ...	2
College of Science ...	306 ...	198

(exclusive of evening students).

As usual, a majority of women take the arts classes in the College of Science. Several women students are now working to obtain degrees. The Principal of the College of Science writes: "We have reason to believe that we have solved the problem of woman's education in a satisfactory manner. We have opened everything to women, without a single exception." This includes the B.Mus. and D.Mus.

Mason College was founded by Sir Josiah Mason in 1875, and formally opened in 1880. It is one of eleven

Mason College, Birmingham, 1875. university colleges which share in the Government grant of £15,000 per annum. The deed of foundation

only provided for scientific instruction, but the scheme
was extended to embrace medicine and the arts.   This
wide curriculum is one that best suits women's interests,
and accordingly we find their numbers very large.   Out
of a total of 690 students for 1895–96, 323 are women.
Birmingham is one of the most advanced educational
centres in England ; the Royal Education Commissioners
(1894–95) drew attention to the fact that the demand
for Secondary Education for girls was practically the
same as for boys in this city.   There are day training
departments for elementary teachers of both sexes
attached to Mason College, and the Council are now
erecting buildings to accommodate 90 women teachers.
Women are prepared for the Preliminary Scientific
Examinations (M.B.) of London University, but the
Medical Faculty is closed to them.   On inquiry as to
the reason, the Secretary replies that exclusion is due
to custom and want of accommodation.

Nottingham University College is largely a result of
the University Extension movement, and, as might be
Nottingham   expected, makes no distinction of
University   religion, as many colleges proudly
College, 1880.   boast, or of sex.   There are 1580
individual students, the sexes tending to approximate in
numbers.   The College has been extended to meet the
needs of this great army of students.   Its governing body
is largely composed of town councillors, the Corporation
having, indeed, built the College, the condition on
which it received an endowment of £10,000.   Much
of its work is of a technical character, and it receives

a grant for this purpose from the Local Taxation Surplus (Customs and Excise Duties Act), 1890.

Firth College was founded in 1879 by Mr. Mark Firth, and was originally intended as a hall and lecture-rooms for the work of the University Extension movement. It required to be extended in 1892, and arrange-ments are now completed for extending it once more by means of an art department. It has besides recently taken over a medical school, an old-standing institution of the town; this is closed to women, although the objects of the College state that "its doors are open to all, without distinction of sex or class." Like Nottingham, Firth College provides higher education by university methods, and by a system of technical instruction makes special provision for local wants. It is partly rate-supported under the Technical Instruction Act of 1889, and receives funds from the Local Taxation Act, as well as a Government grant. The total number of individual students is 325, of whom 88 are women. Both Nottingham and Firth Colleges have day training colleges for men and women teachers, and earn the grants of the Education Department.

Firth College, Sheffield.

Bristol College was founded to promote the education of both sexes; it closes its medical school to women. Besides 78 medical students it has 464 students in arts and science, of whom 238 are men, 166 women, and 60 women in a day training department. It shares in the Government grant, and has an annual sum from

Bristol College, 1876.

the Town Council for free studentships, under the Customs and Excise Act, 1890.

The condition of the universities during the first half of the century illustrates the tendency of wealthy **University** corporations to grow narrow, exclu- **Extension** sive, inert. In ancient records we **movement.** are struck by the tacit assumption that a university student is necessarily poor; in the more modern records of Oxford and Cambridge the assumption has been that a student ought to be wealthy, and that the universities existed for the wealthy. The foundation of two modern universities — London in 1826 (charter bestowed in 1836), and Durham in 1832 —formed a strong protest against the exclusiveness of the ancient universities. Happily, the latter perceived the danger that threatened them. In 1845 Oxford received an address begging the Hebdomadal Board to adopt measures for the admission of a poorer class to the University; the petitioners even offered assistance in money.* The Oxford University Commission of 1850 discussed four out of seven schemes of University Extension laid before it. Arthur Clough and Mark Pattison argued that there must be a gradual, sure, and large extension of the benefits of university teaching. "I look for the extension of the university to the poor," said one advocate. "Though it may be impossible to bring the masses requiring education to the university," wrote Mr. Sewell to the Vice-Chancellor

---

* See *University Extension : Past, Present, and Future.* By H. J. MACKINDER and M. E. SADLER.

of Oxford in 1850, "may it not be possible to carry the university to them?" And then, on paper, he worked out details of an extension scheme. The universities ruminated on the idea for 17 years. Possibly, the period would have been longer, but a convinced believer in the democratization of the universities, Professor James Stuart, received an invitation to lecture to audiences of women from the North of England Council for Promoting the Higher Education of Women. Mrs. Josephine Butler was the President of the Association ; Miss A. J. Clough, the Secretary. In 1867 Professor Stuart gave courses of eight lectures in four great Northern towns; he made a great point that they should form a course, as he had been "vexed with the insufficiency of the single lecture system." Professor Stuart also introduced the syllabus and weekly papers, which are still features of the University Extension scheme. In the same year he invented the "class" at Rochdale, an adjunct to the lecture intended for further explanation of the subject to an audience of working-men. This was the origin of the University Extension movement as we now know it. In 1871 Professor Stuart addressed an important letter on the subject to resident members of Cambridge University ; the following year a syndicate was appointed to consider the matter. Professor Stuart had a ready answer for every conceivable objection, so that, in 1873, the new **Scheme adopted by Cambridge, 1873.** scheme was formally adopted. Meantime, lectures had been given in several towns to both sexes. In 1876 the

London University Extension was formed to meet the special needs of the metropolis.   In 1878 Oxford began to organize her share in the movement, a share which has grown to be very large.   During the session 1894-95 Cambridge University local lectures have been attended by 10,300 students; Oxford by about 30,000; London by 14,200 (students may be counted more than once in these figures, according to the number of courses taken by them).   The number has rather decreased of recent years, partly because other universities, Durham and Victoria, have taken up the work; partly because Oxford and Cambridge, subsequent to 1890, had a considerable share of the work now done by County and Borough Councils in technical instruction; and partly because of the astonishing growth of provincial colleges in large towns, of polytechnics, and similar institutions.   Natural development has thus somewhat limited the field of University Extension in towns where education is appreciated.   The field is still very large; but a movement of this kind depends greatly upon local initiative.   Many fair-sized towns care nothing about higher, and little about any other sort of education.

Need for local initiative.

Officials connected with the movement are never weary of declaring how much it owes to local secretaries and committees; many of the secretaries are women, who throw themselves into the work with characteristic energy and enthusiasm. Authorities variously estimate the proportions of women to men attending the lectures at from three-fifths to two-thirds. It is worth noting that the sexes are scarcely drawn from the same class : there is a tendency for the women to be sisters of university men, and for the men to belong to a non-university class. Oxford and London have both shown readiness to employ women as lecturers, which has been done to a small extent. In this the Extension Societies are really in advance of public opinion. Mr. M. E. Sadler, late Secretary to the University Extension Delegacy, Oxford, writes apropos of this : " There is no part of our work in which many of us take a greater satisfaction than these efforts to pioneer and to influence opinion as regards the employ-ment of women." The subjects of the lectures cover a wide range, including natural science, history, literature, economics, architecture ; at some centres arrangements are made for studying languages and mathematics. Oxford inclines to courses of six lectures ; London, ten ; Cambridge, twelve. Speaking of the six-lecture course at the University Extension Congress, in 1894, Professor Jebb wittily remarked, "Cambridge keeps the article, but does not recommend it." The advocates of the smaller course may be said to have popularity, of the larger, higher educational value, on their side.

Further developments of the movement are travelling libraries, composed of books recommended by the lecturer ; students' associations, affording help and a degree of continuity ; important summer meetings at both the universities, where hundreds of students, including many teachers, assemble for brief summer courses ; and lastly, a scheme of affiliation to the

universities themselves. The Cambridge summer
meeting of 1896 was attended by about 500; in
1896 Oxford had as summer guests some 653 persons,
about four-fifths of whom were women.

The affiliation scheme is an attempt to secure
sequence in the work, since some of the critics of
Students the University Extension movement
affiliated to the dwell upon the lack of system and
University. continuity. Centres that affiliate to
the university take three years' (*i.e.* six terms') courses
in, say, history, or some group of allied subjects,
besides two terms' work in, say, natural science. But
the sequences, though their educational value is high,
tend to alienate many students; and the finance of
a centre suffers by them. Students in sequence courses
may style themselves students affiliated to the university,
and have their three years' residence at a university
remitted to two years. Cambridge has quite recently
remodelled its examination system. For the future the
sessional certificate will cover the work of two terms, the
system previously adopted by the London University
Extension Society.

A further development of the University Extension
movement is the rise of three colleges, at Reading and
Exeter, in close connection, the former with the Oxford
the latter with the Cambridge movement. A third has
just been founded at Colchester.

The University Extension College at Reading was
founded in 1892, and incorporated in 1896. It was
formed by an amalgamation of the Local University

University Extension College, Reading. Extension Association with the schools of science and art, and is therefore organized in four departments: (1) Natural Science, (2) Literary and Normal, (3) Agricultural, (4) Fine and Applied Art. The College is recognized by the Education Department and Science and Art Department. It is an interesting attempt to co-ordinate and manage, from one central governing body, with committees, a wide scheme of education. The College has about 600 students attending its various courses, and is under the wing of the Oxford Delegacy. Every class in the College, and every society, is open to men and women without distinction; women also sit on the governing body.

A similar and equally successful college is at work at Exeter, with a technical department, art department, **Exeter Technical and University Extension College.** and the usual work of the University Extension movement. The College is a municipalized institution, with a Council representing the chief educational bodies of the town, besides 9 members of the City Council. It is noteworthy that the University Extension movement has so far received no State aid, which is a source of disappointment. It is, of course, a well-known fact that university chests exist in a state of depletion. Yet some of the colleges are very wealthy, especially Christ Church,* Magdalen, Trinity, St. John's.* With the exception of Christ Church and Baliol, which

* See note pp. 123-4 for one source whence the endowment of these colleges was obtained.

M

presented the services of a fellow to the Reading College, they seem to have done very little for the movement. Reasonably they might be expected to assist it, for, so far from the numbers of undergraduates suffering by the movement, as was feared when Professor James Stuart addressed his famous letter to the members of Cambridge University, they have doubled.   Whereas

Increase in numbers of Undergraduates. the undergraduates of both universities numbered only some 3000 in the early part of the century, they now number 6153, or 6557 if we venture to count the women in residence.   Miss Montgomery, to whose organizing ability much of the success of Exeter College is due, published a very interesting article* upon "The Opportunity of the Universities," in which she points out that their real interests coincide with Extension, and that encouragement might assume the form of a few fellowships.

The movement is largely of a missionary nature, and where it is most successful, it appears to end in a college at important centres of population.   From this one might argue that University Extension, as we now think of it, is not meant to live long.   But this is taking too optimistic a view of the average state of education throughout the country.   One may safely affirm that the harvest truly is great, and much of it has still to be garnered.

The lack of colleges in out-of-the-way places, and the necessity for a certain amount of individual attention, are amongst the causes which have led to the establish-

* In the *Oxford University Extension Gazette*, December, 1894.

University
Examination
Postal Institution. ment of University correspondence classes. They are chiefly used for preparation for certain examinations. They were founded in 1882 by an association of tutors, to educate students on University lines by means of correspondence. Another set of correspondence classes arose in 1891, under the name of the University Examination Postal Institution; in 1894 it amalgamated with the original correspondence classes, under the newer name. Tuition by correspondence does not allow of the personal contact of teacher and pupil, nor does it readily admit of the latter at once seeking aid in the difficulties he meets; yet it has considerable advantages of its own, especially from the point of examination successes. The pupil learns to express herself, and has the benefit of an able tutor's hektographed notes. The Postal Institution for 1895–96 had 300 students, of whom three-fourths were women, chiefly working for the Cambridge Higher Local, the examinations of London University, and teachers' certificates.

The leviathan correspondence institution is the University Correspondence College founded in 1887,

University
Correspondence
College. which prepares specially, but not entirely, for the examinations of London University. Every year the college has hundreds of successful candidates at these examinations; in 1894–95, they numbered 777, of whom about a fourth were women. There are also excellent correspondence classes at Edinburgh and Glasgow.

SECTION IV.

Technico=Professional Education

I. The Training of Teachers

WE are indebted to the primary system of the country for the idea that the teacher must be trained.

(a) Elementary. The first trace of training is found in the systems advocated in the end of the last century by Dr. Andrew Bell, when teaching the boys of a military orphan asylum near Madras, and by Joseph Lancaster, who, about the same time, was teaching very successfully crowds of poor children in the Borough Road, London. Both men were educational reformers of their day, and both claimed to be the inventors of the monitorial system, which

The Monitorial System. was simply setting the elder scholars to teach the rest. Lancaster seems to have been genuinely enthusiastic, and success attended his efforts. Powerful patrons, amongst them George III. and the Duke of Bedford, came to his aid, so that in 1804 he was able to open a new building, consisting of a large house and school-room in Belvedere Place, Borough Road. Lancaster issued pamphlets on how to teach 10,000 children to read in three months.

The weak spot of his system, in vogue for almost half a century, was its constant change. In 1846 the Committee of Council remedied this defect by introducing the pupil teacher system, as a development and improvement on the monitorial system. The idea was borrowed from Holland. At the age of thirteen or

Pupil Teachers, 1846. fourteen, children were apprenticed to the head teacher, usually for five years, and were paid for the first year's service £10, rising to £20 for the last year. Head teachers were responsible for the training of the pupil teachers out of school hours, and received a £3 or £4 bonus for each one who passed her yearly examination satisfactorily. For years large numbers of schools were staffed merely by a head teacher, her pupil teachers, and perhaps an assistant; quite a young child would be given 40 children to teach. Usually she learned the lesson of keeping her regiment in order, having, indeed, little else to teach her charges. Shortly before the introduction of the pupil teacher system, in 1839–40, the first training college had been founded at Battersea in connection with the Church of England. In its early days the Committee of Council used to make building grants for the erection of schools, a policy it completely abandoned later on; in 1843 we find it affording aid for the erection of training colleges, and soon the movement was in full swing, especially after the Council began to make quite a handsome payment of £20 or £25 for each pupil teacher who passed an examination known as the Queen's Scholarship Examination, requiring her, if successful, to enter a training college for a two years' course. The sects vied with each other in emulation of the custom of intending teachers, and by 1887 there were in England 44 residential training colleges, of which 30 were connected with the Church of England. To this day the Education Department does not possess a single Government training college; it merely subsidizes sectarian institutions, which are for the most part connected with religious bodies, maintaining a hold over them by means of money grants and inspection. Amongst the best of the colleges for women subsidized by the Education Department are those of Oxford, Stockwell, Tottenham, and Edgehill.

An immense army of elementary teachers is working **Proportion of the** under the Education Dept. Certificated, **Sexes engaged** provisionally certificated, assistant and **in Teaching.** additional teachers number:

			1896		1876
Women	.	.	66,310	...	14,901
Men	.	.	26,270	...	11,616
Total	.	.	92,580	...	26,517

PUPIL TEACHERS.*

			1896		1876
Girls	.	.	26,757	...	19,436
Boys	.	.	7,245	...	11,102
				...	
Total	.	.	34,002	...	30,538

* An official announcement was made on January 12th, 1897, that the Lord President of the Council, the Duke of Devonshire, has appointed a committee to inquire into the working of the pupil-teacher system in England and Wales. Of its ten members, three are women.

The difference in the numbers of pupil teachers is not so great as in the case of adult teachers, but the altered proportion of the sexes is most striking.

The following tables show that a higher percentage of trained teachers is to be found among men than among women. The report refers to 14,275 schools examined in a year previous to 1895:

	MEN per cent.		WOMEN. per cent.
Trained for two years . .	67·26	...	47·04
Trained for less than two years .	3·53	...	2·19
Untrained	29·21	...	50·77

Studying in the 44 different residential training colleges we find 3,492 individuals, of whom 2,269 are

Numbers of Students in Training Colleges. in colleges connected with the Church of England; 888 are to be found in the 14 day training colleges, which have recently sprung up in various towns. These colleges are strictly unsectarian, and their comparatively rapid increase is significant. They are connected with the Welsh colleges, the colleges of Victoria University, Firth College, London University, King's College, the Universities of Oxford and Cambridge, Mason College, Nottingham University College, Bristol and other colleges. The supply of trained teachers is not equal to the demand, and everything seems to point to the necessity of the Department taking up the work itself, at least to some extent.

It is admitted on all hands that what the student of an elementary training college knows, that she can usually teach. On the other hand, it is urged that the culture of the students is very narrow; even one foreign language is not obligatory upon students in training colleges, though a majority of the women take French.

The Education Department draws a most singular distinction between the cost of a man's education in a training college and a woman's. It pays for the education of a man £50 per annum to his college; for a woman, £35. This is as if the Department assessed the value of the sexes thus:

MAN.	WOMAN.
1	·7

If this is really their respective values, it is certainly incompatible with a high and generous educational policy to use the services of women so largely as the Department does. This rate of pay would seem to be maintained throughout, for if we turn to the average salaries of a master and mistress, we shall find that of the former to be £122 6s. 7d.; the latter, £81 3s. 3d. It is sometimes stated that women need to retire earlier from the teaching profession than men do. The "waste" in women teachers is undoubtedly greater than in men; the Department loses of its trained teachers 4 per cent. men, 6⅛ women. Women could hardly therefore reasonably expect exactly the same pay as men; if they must retire earlier, they would need to take a less reward. But it is doubtful whether School Boards, managers, and all those who pay teachers,

Question of the Teachers' pay; Men and Women compared.

accepting the assessment of the Department for the training colleges, have hit upon the right proportion in giving a third less pay to women, especially as women often prepare sewing in their leisure, instead of enjoying reasonable recreation. School Boards and other employers of teachers in this respect treat women as if they were stronger than men. Men's better physique allows them to work in a far greater proportion in the evening continuation schools, for which of course they are paid extra. We are certainly in great need of comparative health tables, shewing what the difference between the sexes actually amounts to. Women have suffered far too much in the past by guesses at their inefficiency in one field and another, on which are based regulations affecting their well-being.

Yet poor as we may think women's payment to-day, there is little doubt that it is steadily improving. The Select Committee of the House of Commons, which sat upon the education of the poorer classes in 1838, elicited some curious information under this head. The Rev. James Cotton Wigram stated in his evidence that the National Society had men and women, between twenty-two and thirty years of age, training for teachers in the Society's schools. It paid the men 10s. 6d. weekly for giving instruction after they had proved their competence, whereas the women got nothing at all but a small gratuity on leaving. They had to pay for their own board whilst teaching.

As is shewn later, the Science and Art Department undertakes the inspection of the drawing of students

The Science
and Art
Department.

in training colleges. They receive credit for passing in the Department's examinations in science, women chiefly affecting such subjects as physiology, botany, physiography, and hygiene. Their total number of science passes obtained in the previous May, for which they received credit at the Christmas examination, 1895, was 1498, as compared with 855 men. Colleges are beginning to attach more importance to physical training than ever before, but are still largely indifferent to recreation for women, even although the means of recreation is provided. There is probably a good deal of truth in the accusation, that women in training colleges, both in England and abroad, are overworked; they have too often that appearance. The importance to their future career of a good place in their final examinations, the fact that women who are in training are at a delicate age, that almost immediately after they leave college they take up responsible work where they must shew their value, all go to prove the desirability of slackening competition, of giving, in colleges subsidized by Government, the highest grant only where physique is good.

(b) *Training for Secondary Teachers*

Training for secondary teachers directly resulted from primary training. Women are leading in this branch of

The Home and
Colonial School
Society, 1836.

education, and it is credibly stated that this is the only branch in which they do lead. The Home and

Colonial School Society, which was founded to give effect to the views of Pestalozzi, especially as regards the teaching of infants, first began to train infant teachers for elementary schools in 1836, and then extended the training to nursery governesses and teachers of secondary schools. For more than thirty years this Society was the only body offering secondary teachers any sort of training. These latter students, numbering about forty, used to practise in elementary day schools. In particular, a considerable number of teachers for mission schools were at one time trained in the college in Gray's Inn Road. In 1895, the non-Government department removed to Highbury Hill House, as a secondary and kindergarten training college for women teachers, where students have now a secondary school in which to practise. It still remains a branch of the Home and Colonial School Society.

The Maria Grey was really the first training college in the field, an outcome of the energy of the Teachers' **Maria Grey** Training and Registration Society. **Training College,** The Society was formed in 1877, **1878.** largely as a result of the efforts of Mrs. Wm. Grey, and her sister, Miss Shirreff. Next year the training college was opened at Bishopsgate in connection with a middle-class girls' school, which the Rev. Wm. Rogers placed at its disposal. It removed to Fitzroy Street in 1885, and to-day the training college and a high school have admirable premises in the same building at Brondesbury, with Miss Woods as principal. The college is non-residential; its work divides into three parts, lower, higher, and kindergarten. The Council of the Teachers' Training and Registration, recognizing how much women's education suffers by lack of endowment, have often rendered assistance in money to earnest students in need of it; the members are justly proud that, although under no obligation to do so, women who have benefited by it have in some cases refunded the money, unasked, in order that others might reap the same advantage.

The establishment of the Cambridge Teachers' Certificate Examination in 1878 has given an un-**The Cambridge** doubted stimulus to the training of **Teachers' Train-** teachers, at least among women; most **ing Syndicate,** training colleges, or training depart-**1878.** ments in connection with colleges, aim at this diploma for their students. The certificates of the Teachers' Training Syndicate are now held by 50 men and 941 women. The Secretary of the Syndicate reports a gradual increase of numbers both among men and women. The examination instituted by the Syndicate covers the history, theory, and practice of education, and is intended for persons who have previously shewn intellectual qualifications in passing one of several specified University examinations.

It was reserved for a younger and sister College of the Maria Grey to boldly plant itself in a University town. **Cambridge Train-** In Miss Ridley's *Frances Mary Buss* **ing College for** she tells us how Miss Buss was wishful **Women, 1885.** to have the Maria Grey associated with the North London Collegiate School, when it became a question of removing the College from Bishopsgate. This fell through; but seeing how the students of Girton and Newnham entered the teaching profession by the hundred without training, Miss Buss, Mrs. Bryant, and a number of educationists, both men and women, determined that there should be a training college at the very gates of the University. The College began its work in some cottages near Newnham, and finally removed to a commodious and suitable building in 1895. It trains sixty students for one year; they obtain their practice in some fourteen elementary and secondary schools, with about 1700 pupils. Miss E. P. Hughes, herself a distinguished student of Newnham, is the principal. The Council rightly attach great importance to the year's residence at Cambridge; for though the Universities can hardly be called effusive or eager when a new development arises, yet Cambridge has rendered excellent service to the cause of training teachers, and there are substantial advantages to be reaped by residence in the town.

Miss Beale, of Cheltenham, early recognized the necessity for training women as secondary teachers.

Training Department at the Ladies' College, Cheltenham. Since 1885 the Ladies' College has had a definite training department, the students boarding at a hostel, St. Hilda's, and receiving all their instruction at the College. There are two divisions in the training department: (*a*) Some fifteen secondary teachers, under Miss Louch, almost all working for the Cambridge Teachers' Certificate; (*b*) A kindergarten department, under Miss Welldon, in which fifty students prepare for the Higher Froebel Certificate. Practice is obtained in the College, and in neighbouring schools, especially the Kindergarten at St. Stephen's, managed entirely by Miss Welldon. At St. Hilda's, twenty foundationers are accepted for training on lower terms, with the proviso that they devote themselves to teaching. These are, practically, scholarships given to those who require them most, or will use them to the best advantage.

The Datchelor Training College is in connection with the Mary Datchelor School for Girls, Camberwell, of which it is an outgrowth. The College is non-residential, and by its constitution the numbers may not exceed 26. Besides obtaining practice in the Mary Datchelor School, the students give lessons in a large London Board school near the College. Miss C. Rigg is principal both of the Datchelor School and College.

Datchelor Training College, 1888.

Men have so far shewn themselves very chary of patronising training in the teacher's art. A training college once existed for them in Cowper Street, but died of inanition. The College of Preceptors is making a praiseworthy effort, at great expense, to revive such a college. It was opened in October, 1895, but so far the College has experienced the truth of Professor Sully's observation in the *Journal of Education* (June, 1894), that the head-masters of English secondary schools, when engaging an assistant, think more of a good bat or a good degree than of necessary training. In this connection it is worth observing that the College of Preceptors has for many years given teachers' courses of useful lectures, on the art of teaching and kindred subjects, by eminent educationists, which have been largely used by those whose work would not allow of training within the walls of a college. The Council have besides offered four scholarships at training colleges, both to men and women.

But though men fight shy of training colleges, they avail themselves, to some extent, of the opportunities

Training encouraged at University Colleges. of day training now afforded in many large towns and educational centres, in the local university colleges at Aberystwyth, Cardiff, and other places. Girton and Newnham seem rather to have adopted the masculine attitude towards training: the degree or equivalent of a degree is enough—the teacher is heaven-sent. So much nonsense continues to be talked on the subject, usually by men and women who pass straight from the university colleges to the class-room, that it may be pardonable to point out that those who dispense with training are not even in as good a position as men and women who have passed medical examinations and have omitted to walk the hospitals under trained guidance. The medical student never quite loses sight of the hospital; the undergraduate need never cross the threshold of a school. Occasionally a comparison is instituted between the untrained graduate and some trained, insufficiently educated person. This is scarcely ingenuous; the only fair comparison must be drawn between the trained graduate and the untrained. It is said that there is a tendency for those who lack degrees to atone by training. Even if this were so, it could not remain as a permanent condition, when thorough equipment and specialization are so much to the front.

A House of Education at Ambleside was opened in 1892 for the training of thirty primary (*i.e.* for young **Training for** children) and secondary governesses, **Private** under Miss Charlotte M. Mason. The **Governesses.** course has recently been extended to two years, and is such as to enable young women to discharge the duties of such posts thoroughly well. The House is an outcome of the Parents' National Educational Union, which, with its twenty-two active branches in London and the country, makes a successful effort to place ideals and schemes of education before that individual whom other educational societies find so unreachable, the British parent. Miss Mason has made a praiseworthy effort to induce mothers to take up a three years' educational course; already 62 mothers have become members. The significance of the movement can scarcely be over-estimated; the idea it embodies is bound to spread.

The National Froebel Union is formed by the union of three societies, the Froebel Society (1874), Kinder- **National Froebel** garten Company, and Home and **Union.** Colonial School Society, for certificate purposes. Certificates are not now issued by these separate societies, but by the Joint Examination Board of the Froebel Union; the Education Department recognizes them. There are no statistics as to the number of kindergarten teachers; but it is worth noting that the Froebel Society issued 72 certificates down to 1887; the Froebel Union, from 1887–1895, issued 884 (sometimes an individual holds two certificates). In 1896 almost 600 candidates sat for the examinations. The Kindergarten Company and Home and Colonial School Society have training colleges for students. Of recent years there has been a great and growing demand for kindergarten teachers, especially among high schools and private schools. The elementary infant schools of the country, especially the Voluntary schools, are said to have, very rarely, true and properly equipped kindergartens. The work of the Froebel Society is intended to promote co-operation amongst those engaged in kindergarten work, and to spread the knowledge of Froebel's methods of education.

II. London School of Medicine for Women.

If we wish to know the reason why the London School of Medicine, modestly housed in a private dwelling in Handel Street, Brunswick Square, was founded, we must seek it in the Northern capital. In 1869 Miss Jex-Blake and some other women students matriculated in medicine at Edinburgh University, one **Attempt to obtain** of the most important medical schools **Teaching at** in the kingdom. The governing body **Edinburgh.** were quite willing that women should

N

take medical degrees; but, unhappily, the professors held different views on woman's sphere. The ladies were insulted in the streets of Edinburgh by under-graduates whose prejudices outran their knowledge and discretion; students even went the length of throwing missiles at those who offended their sense of propriety. Miss Jex-Blake was unsuccessful in her attempts in the Scottish Law Courts to compel the professors to carry out the instructions of the governing body of Edinburgh University. Edinburgh was abandoned, and the attack concentrated upon London.

Mrs. Garrett Anderson, M.D., already in practice with a Paris degree, Dr. Anstie, Dr. King Chambers, Mrs. Thorne, and many others were willing and able to help. Anstie was most enthusiastic, and in a few weeks the Henrietta Street School was organized, with a large and important staff of lecturers, and twenty-three students. As an illustration of the poverty against which women have so often to contend, it is noteworthy that the new medical school began operations with little more than £1000. It is a long story how hospital committees were ready to welcome women students, but the medical staff, bent on the protection of their interests, invariably refused admission to the wards. Dr. T. Chambers, of Chelsea, gave the Women's Medical School permission to enter some wards of Chelsea Hospital, and a little more practice was obtained at the New Hospital for Women. Thanks to the tact and energy of Mr. Jas. Stansfeld, and Mr. Hopgood, Chairman of the Committee of the Royal Free Hospital, Gray's Inn

Road, women were ultimately admitted to the wards of that hospital, on condition that they paid a yearly subsidy of £315 to the funds of the hospital. This was remitted at the end of five years, the school guaranteeing £400 per annum to the medical staff for the first five years, and £460 for the next five years. Though the premises of the London School of Medicine leave much to be desired, the teaching given is second to none, the professors being of high standing. At present, there are 150 women studying medicine in the school, about half of whom are working for the degrees of London University. Women may obtain teaching at University College for the preliminary scientific M.B. examination; members of such classes are counted as science students. Other medical training at University College is closed to them, as it is at Owens College, Liverpool College, Yorkshire College, Mason College of Science, Nottingham University College, Firth College, Sheffield, and Bristol College. In some cases, only clinical instruction is not obtainable for women students.

Examinations of London University are open to them, and they already hold these degrees:

Bachelor of Medicine	53
Doctor of Medicine	15
Bachelor of Surgery	10
Master of Surgery	1

Students work not only for the degrees of London University, but for those of the Royal University of Ireland, the Irish and Scotch Colleges of Physicians and Surgeons, for Durham, Glasgow, and Edinburgh.

Some 212 women on the medical register have obtained the whole or part of their training at the London School; about 77 others are on the register who did not obtain their training here.

It is advisable to allude here to a movement now on foot for definite training of medical nurses. At present, "trained and certificated nurse" means a great many different things, for lack of a uniform standard. Each hospital seems to have its own standard, a system that gives rise to considerable trouble. Mrs. Bedford Fenwick advocates a definite collegiate curriculum for the education of nurses.

III. *Science and Art Department, South Kensington.*

Allusion has already been made to the work of the Science and Art Department in elementary schools and **Science and Art** in secondary education generally, the **Department,** latter part of its work being very **S. Kensington.** various. The Department has long recognized the necessity for training teachers to take up its work both in science and art, and this training is extended to others who pay its fees, or win their way to the centre by means of a system of exhibitions and scholarships. It was found to be one thing to be able to pass the examinations of the Department, and another to be an able and successful teacher.

The Normal School of Science was established in 1859; in 1881 it was entirely reorganized, and the Royal (*d*) **Royal College of Science.** School of Mines incorporated with it; in 1890 its title was changed to the Royal College of Science. Its sessional courses were attended during the first part of the session 1896–97 by 300 men and 6 women. The course at the Royal College of Science lasts three years, and those who pass through it in a prescribed order receive the title of Associate. Besides these regular students, who are very largely the successful candidates of the spring examinations, teachers of scientific subjects in elementary and other schools have ever since 1868 been encouraged to come to London for a short scientific summer course in a branch of science they teach or wish to teach. Their third-class return railway fare is paid to South Kensington, and each receives a bonus of £3 towards incidental expenses. Of course, great stress is laid upon practical work in the laboratories; 202 men and 10 women availed themselves of the help thus afforded by the Department in 1894–95.

The subjects most popular with women are botany, physiology, and hygiene; but, as the figures shew, women scarcely avail themselves of the admirable opportunities placed within their reach.

It is quite otherwise with the Art Department, for in the training school women are in a slight majority.

The Royal College of Art. The college is a development of the School of Design and Central School of Art at Somerset House, created in 1837, and at that time under the control of the Board of Trade. An important feature of the work has

always been the training of teachers. The title of
School of Design was altered in 1852 to Department
of Science and Art, and the location changed to Marlborough House. When the Education Department was
constituted in 1856, the Science and Art Department
to a certain extent amalgamated with it, and both were
placed under the Lord President and Vice-President of
Council. In 1857 the Science and Art Department
removed to South Kensington. The fate of the Royal
Female School of Art is treated later.

There is no special difference in the treatment of
the sexes as regards privileges. The cost of their art
Women not Head education is reckoned to be the same ;
Teachers in Local but, as far as scholarships are con-
Schools of Art. cerned, the number of women is much
smaller. The students in training for the post of head
of a local art school are men. Such appointments rest
with local committees, and no woman seems yet to
have convinced a locality that she could assume such
a position. There seems no reason whatever why a
woman should not be a head teacher in the schools
of the Department, since she occasionally now works
as an assistant, and it is for women to note how
they suffer when excluded, and they practically are
excluded, by local opinion, from some of the most
highly considered posts of the profession. It has been
pointed out that in the immense lists of teachers' names
in the calendar of the Science and Art Department,
1896, pp. 2–412, there might be a woman's name. But
even if this were so, the contention would not be

affected. Men reasonably claim the highest creative power in art, but such power is frequently incompatible with the work of a teacher. Mr. Walter Crane, on resigning his post of Director of the Manchester Municipal School of Art, in July 1896, shewed how difficult it is to dovetail work and teaching. It would seem to be wisdom on the part of women to obtain seats on local committees, so that their sex may not be passed over by default. The Department is not always well served by its men teachers, and it would be difficult to maintain that, in teaching, efficiency is limited to one sex.

It is only fair to add that the Department has recently employed women as examiners in the National Art Competition with success. There are twenty-three art subjects in which instruction may be obtained at an art school. The training at the Central School of Art, which contains a large proportion of the picked scholars of local art schools, lasts about two years for women, four for men. There is good reason to suppose that as far as design is concerned, women show more invention, fancy, and adaptability than men, but less power to endure sustained effort. The sexes work together in the different departments. Holders of scholarships work for about 40 weeks in the year, and receive a weekly sum of 25*s.* from the Department for maintenance. In the art section, the Department is more and more using inspection as a means of assessing its grants to local art schools. It also superintends the work of 4484 persons in training colleges for elementary teachers subsidized by the Education Department.

Number of Students in the National Art Training School,
South Kensington, 1896.
Total, 479.

					Men.		Women.
Total	.	.	.	.	238	...	241
National Scholars	.	.	.		72	...	14
Free Students	.	.	.		34	...	43
Local Scholars	.	.	.		8	...	4

The Royal Female School of Art stands on a different footing from other metropolitan schools of art: it is

Royal Female School of Art, Queen Square, W.C., 1842. really an offshoot of the School of Design which preceded the Science and Art Department. The School of Design was originally located at Somerset House, in 1842-43, under the Board of Trade; the women's section was managed besides by a committee of artists. In 1853 the School of Design removed to Marlborough House, with the exception of the women students, who found a home in Gower Street, and afterwards in Queen Square, under the control of the Science and Art Department. Though not architecturally beautiful, as one would prefer art schools to be, the premises are commodious, and an excellent training is obtained by more than a hundred students, under Miss Louisa Gann, who has been connected with the school since the day it was founded. The school enjoys royal patronage, and many beautiful designs have been produced for the members of the royal family at different times. The course of training usually lasts from three to five years, and embraces painting in oil and water-colour, drawing from the life and from the antique, design, illustration, modelling in clay and wax.

Many valuable scholarships exist in connection with the school, and are annually competed for. In the lithographic studio women receive technical instruction in the new art printing processes, one of the greatest art developments of the day. The work of the studio is admirable, and is said to be equal to the best German processes.

IV. *Music.*

It was Liszt who, critically observing the indiscriminating appreciation of a London concert hall, remarked: "The English would applaud me if I sat on the piano." Yet though musicians have still to complain of lack of musical culture, much has been done in recent years to raise the standard. Indeed, it is a question deserving the attention of those interested whether the national taste did not sink very low because of the low condition of women's education. Music was not loved and studied for itself, but as a mere accomplishment, an added string to the bow of attractiveness.

Various bodies have helped to raise the standard. First, in point of time, is the Royal Academy of Music.

Royal Academy of Music, 1823. The Academy began its work in 1823 with twenty students; to-day it has 500; in all, some 6000 persons have received a part, or the whole, of their training by its means. Ensemble practice, sight-reading, orchestral and operatic work, languages, and instruction in a large number of instruments, form part of the curriculum. The Academy has done good work by means of its system of examinations, which used to be held all over the country in the spring, and which have largely helped to wipe out the ineffectual pretence at teaching music which was common a generation ago. It has helped to substitute a very fair standard in theory and performance. In 1889 the Academy united with the Royal College of Music, under the title of the Associated Board, for the purpose of maintaining these provincial examinations. It still carries on in

The Associated Board, 1889. London its metropolitan examination for teachers and performers, who hold the title of Fellow or Associate. It is worthy of note that the Associated Board publishes a register of schools and individual teachers whose standard is satisfactory. Less satisfactory, unless there is some reasonable explanation for it, is the list of the professional staff, where, out of 94 teachers, only four are women, and of these three for singing : not one out of 24 pianoforte teachers is a woman. Beneath is a list of "sub-professors," in which women are plentiful enough. This is the more remarkable, as among the Academy's list of famous scholars women's names are by no means scarce.

The Guildhall School of Music was founded in 1880 by the Corporation of the City of London, and has its

The Guildhall School of Music, 1880. home in a convenient building on Victoria Embankment. The fees are more moderate than in some schools of music, with the result that the numbers have rushed up from 65 in 1880 to 3700 in 1896. Of these, three-fourths are women, both amateurs and professionals. There are 46 scholarships, open to both sexes, offered to those who have studied at least three terms in the school. Besides which, certificates, medals, prizes stimulate the students to work. About forty instruments and subjects are taught by a very large mixed staff, and there are an orchestra, a choir, and an operatic class.

Another body which is doing good work to advance the cultivation of music is the Royal College. It was founded by the exertions of the Prince of Wales, incorporated in 1883, and removed to handsome buildings near the Albert Hall in 1894. In 1896 the Royal College had 324 pupils. Of these, 263 were paying students, 205 being women; of 61 holding scholarships, 16 were women. Scholarships are gained by competition, open to all classes and both sexes, unless the donor stipulates otherwise. At Easter, the College holds an examination for its Associateship (A.R.C.M.), also open to both sexes, an honour which women often obtain.

Royal College of Music, 1883.

Good authorities, in answer to a query addressed to them touching improvement in musical culture, have replied that this improvement is very marked, especially during the last decade. One enthusiastic amateur attributes it to facilities for foreign travel, enabling people to judge of Continental standards; to the Saturday and Monday Popular Concerts, and those of the Crystal Palace; and to the well-known work of the late Sir Charles Hallé in the North. Allusion has already been made to the work of the Royal College, associated with the Royal Academy, in its system of examinations; the effect of these has been very notable.

In some schools, notably the Cheltenham Ladies' College, great attention is paid to music, and the results are distinctly good. In the elementary training colleges attention is given to vocal music, the inspectors of the Education Department attaching importance to its cultivation.

Trinity College was founded in 1872 as a voluntary musical society; in 1881 it received a new and amended constitution, whereby its sphere of usefulness was largely extended. Its scholarships are offered on the ground of absolute equality between the sexes. Quite recently women have been appointed on the professorial staff.

Trinity College, 1881.

Trinity College has its own scheme of examinations, including Matriculation, Associate in Music, Licentiate in Music, and Fellowship.

V. *Three Technical Colleges for Women.*

It has been said that as an influence which makes for morality, good cookery has never yet been sufficiently reckoned with. However this may be, it is certain that the National School of Cookery is doing a great and a needed work. The school is an outcome of

The National School of Cookery, 1873.

a series of lectures delivered at the International Exhibition of 1872 by Mr. J. C. Buckmaster, of the Science and Art Department. It was computed that 250,000 persons attended these lectures, illustrated by four women cooks, and this fact seemed to show the need for methodical and scientific instruction.

The following year the School of Cookery was called into existence; ever since the Duke of Westminster has remained President of the School; the Hon. E. F. Leveson-Gower, the Chairman of Committee; and, with the exception of the first year, Mrs. Charles Clarke has been the superintendent. The School very courageously worked for its capital to build new premises, those it occupied at South Kensington up to 1889 being far from suitable. It had the management of the cheap dinners at a series of Exhibitions, the Fisheries, Health, Inventions, Colonial, and Indian; by this means, and as a result of the able management providing good food at cheap rates, the School of Cookery saved £5000. With this it built its handsome premises in Buckingham Palace Road. They consist of an excellent series of kitchens for giving lessons to children from elementary schools; cooks studying artizan, middle-class, and high-class cooking; rooms for laundry work, dressmaking, and millinery. Since its foundation the School has granted 1305 diplomas; this by no means covers its field of usefulness. Large numbers of ladies attend classes, especially ladies on the eve of their marriage; when the London season opens, girls come for parts of the course that attract them, and cooks also work up certain departments. The diploma really means that the holder is qualified to teach cookery; and, as a result of the efforts of the original institution, large numbers of towns have cookery schools of their own, with properly qualified instructors. It is well known that to-day a good elementary school cannot earn the higher grant without domestic economy as a subject. The London School Board was, in its early days, approached by the Committee of the School of Cookery, and the development of its course of instruction was influenced and assisted by the School of Cookery. An arrangement was made with the Education Department, by which the School granted local diplomas to students in training colleges and pupil teachers in elementary schools. The Government grant of 4s. per head was earned by 7000 children in 1883, by 90,000 in 1892. Circumstances compelled the Cookery School to widen its curriculum. Under its roof can now be obtained a course of instruction in laundry work, as well as in home dressmaking and millinery, so that the real title of this useful institution should be School of Domestic Economy. The School has had the honour of advising the War Office authorities how to improve sick cookery in military hospitals, messing in the army; it has sent instructors to the Army School of Cookery, has helped in Volunteer cookery instruction, and in the movement set on foot by the Admiralty to train navy cooks. It assisted to organize classes to train the nurses of the London Hospitals in cookery for the sick.

A diploma of plain cookery costs about £20; high-class cookery, £21. It should be distinctly understood that the holder of a diploma is not only a practical cook, but able to undertake class teaching and teaching by demonstration. The County Councils of London, Kent, and Surrey grant about a dozen scholarships of the value of £10 10s. each. Unhappily these have rather a way of working themselves into the hands of those for whom they were scarcely intended, the vicar's relatives, for instance. The upper rooms of the School are used for boarding ladies; rooms in the basement for cooks and holders of artizan scholarships.

The School suffers from a difficulty in disposing of its cooked food; recently it has made an effort to make known that dishes are for sale. It has and requires a large and expensive staff of teachers for its numerous activities. It desires aid from the Technical Education Board, which hitherto it has not obtained. It has also to bear a very heavy ground rental of £210 per annum. No doubt its able management can reflect upon rent as that "delicate alchemy by which the perfumed seigneur can extract every fourth nettle from the widow's pot." The ground rent of the School, its rates, coal, and gas, amount to more than £700 per annum. It subsists solely on its fees and subscriptions of a few friends, who give one vote for every £1 subscribed towards training a student, instead of her paying the fees.

The Physical Training College at Dartford Heath owes its inception to a Swedish lady, Mme. Bergman

Physical Training College, 1885. Oesterberg, who came to London in 1881, and received the appointment of physical trainer under the London School Board. For some years Mme. Oesterberg worked at the training of the Board's teachers, some thousand of whom passed through her hands. It is not always known that the yearly demonstration of school children, which takes place in the Albert Hall in July, is managed by those whose training was received under Mme. Oesterberg. But the results at which Ling's Swedish system aims, the careful graduation of exercises to suit the student's strength and the development of the muscles with due regard to symmetry, can hardly be obtained by a weekly exercise of an hour's duration, often performed in an unsuitable, and even injurious costume, at a time when the pupil may be fatigued. Personal health and hygienic surroundings, diet, clothing, regulation of the hours of rest and work, all require consideration. To this end the Hampstead Physical Training College was founded in 1885 to prepare students of Ling's system to undertake work in schools and colleges as gymnastic teachers. The course, which lasts two years, embraces gymnastics according to Ling's system, physiology, hygiene, anatomy, medical massage, elementary pathology, ambulance. In addition, students thoroughly learn such games as lawn tennis, cricket, hockey, basket ball, as well as cycling and dancing, with the aim of introducing games and recreation into girls' schools and colleges as a regular part of the curriculum. The

College has proved highly successful, removing in 1895 to larger premises and beautiful grounds of some fourteen acres. Every year more schools make arrangements for the physical education of their pupils; indeed, the chief reason why greater progress has not been made, is that teachers adopt poor systems because of their inability to distinguish between them and Ling's.

To many who hold the opinion, or at least fear, that without some greatly needed reform in dress, and an improvement in physique and muscular development, the mental activities and social usefulness of women are hampered and depressed, the movement here briefly indicated is of special interest and significance. It is useless to deny that women's higher education has still its inveterate foes, who are only too ready to proclaim that deterioration of physique follows upon the mental application required by a college course. So recently as 1887 Mrs. Henry Sidgwick, the well-known principal of Newnham College, prepared an elaborate series of health statistics of past and present women students at Cambridge and Oxford, and of their sisters, from which she concluded that "there is nothing in a university education at all specially injurious to the constitution of women or involving any greater strain than they can ordinarily bear without injury," and that "women generally pass through it without its affecting their health one way or the other." Mrs. Sidgwick in comparing the health of college students and their sisters nearest in age who had not been to college, found that "during college life 5 per cent. more students had excellent or good health, and 5 per cent. fewer had poor or bad health than sisters between 18 and 21." Other tables (in all there are 41 elaborate statistical tables) go on to show that the children of married students are healthier, and have a lower death-rate, than those of sisters; so that although it must be set down as a fact unfavourable to the university education of women that there is a temporary falling off during college life of about 5 per cent. in good health, as compared with either health at entering or at the time statistics were taken, depending to some extent on the relaxing climate of the universities, alarm on the score of health is groundless. The publication of this pamphlet,* able and impartial as it undoubtedly is, gave satisfaction to the women engaged in education.

Yet most women, one might say all who have reflected upon the subject, are convinced that improvement in the health of their sex is a consideration second to none. Such improvement can never follow as a result of either physical or mental indolence, but must proceed on the lines of rational and regulated exercise, coupled with healthy and enjoyable games, and an improved dress. Some devotees of this faith do not hesitate to say that if only one of the sexes should enjoy this exercise, and aim at higher physical development, that sex should be the weaker one. The consideration of so important

* *Health Statistics of Women Students of Cambridge and Oxford, and of their Sisters.* By Mrs. HENRY SIDGWICK. Cambridge University Press, 1890. 1s. 6d.

a matter is, perhaps, not out of place in a work on women's education; and since one outcome of reflection and of anxiety on the subject has been the foundation and the hearty support of a college of physical education, to chronicle it has been a duty. Mme. Bergman Oesterberg's Physical Training College shares with the Royal Central Institute of Gymnastics in Stockholm the distinction of being the only college in Europe in which a full course of instruction is given in the theory and practice of the Swedish system, differing from the Institute in the importance ascribed to games, and the position given them in the curriculum.

Swanley Horticultural College was founded in 1888 for men, the question of a women's department never

Swanley Horticultural College— Women's Department, 1891. appearing to occur to the founders. The idea of extending its benefits to women is due to Miss Cons, who, not long after her election to the London County Council, when it conferred upon her the dignity of Alderman, had occasion to visit some homes for little boys at Swanley, under the direction of the L.C.C. Miss Cons on that occasion also saw over the Swanley Horticultural College, which was at that time somewhat of the nature of a private enterprise. The possibility of its further development, both for men and women, struck Miss Cons as great. She and a friend entered the College as students, satisfied themselves that the occupation was in all respects suitable for women, and forthwith took steps to begin a women's branch, which ever since has been increasingly successful. A large council of influential persons was formed ; a committee of thirteen chosen, of whom twelve are ladies, and in 1891 a house secured, about five minutes' walk from the College.   The committee were fortunate in their choice of a Lady Superintendent ; for not a little of the success of the new branch is due to Mrs. Watson's care and organizing ability.   In the autumn of 1896, there were twenty-eight women students working at the College, a number slightly in excess of the men.   But for this development on the women's side, as well as for aid afforded by County Councils, it is not certain that the work of the College could have continued at all.   Its expenses are very heavy, it was at that time not very well known, and the smallness of its numbers greatly minimised its usefulness in every way.   The twenty-eight students are composed of ladies who adopt gardening as a means of making a livelihood ; others who train themselves in order to manage their own gardens, or assume oversight in their homes ; and, thirdly, by County Council scholars who find their way to the College by the arrangements of Technical Instruction Committees. The three County Councils of London, Kent, and Essex offer scholarships both to men and women.   In addition, the Ladies' Committee of Swanley College have hitherto provided funds for two different scholar- ships to be held at the College.   The fees for women are from £70 to £86.

The college course divides itself into practical and theoretical work.   The forty-three acres of ground on which students practise, contain fruit orchards, vegetable and flower gardens, and immense glass houses. Scientific horticulture includes the selection, management, pruning, and grafting of fruit trees; how different bush fruits should be combined in an orchard; culture under glass; gathering, packing, marketing, preserving of fruits either in water or by sugar or evaporation; production of early vegetables, hybridization and propagation, seeds and sowing, preparation of soils, digging, ploughing, draining, trenching, paring, etc.; manures, their composition and modes of application.

The theoretical work comprises a knowledge of botany, chemistry, geology, physics, building construction, measuring, levelling, and so forth. Students are besides given lessons in bee-keeping, poultry-farming, dairying, table decoration, bouquet making. Besides a lecture theatre and class-rooms, students share in common a small physical laboratory and library.

VI. *Technical Instruction.*

In England there have seldom been lacking cultured individuals who have steadfastly maintained that education is neither for one sex, nor for a leisured and cultured class, but for all. Sunday schools and ragged schools attest the practical outcome of this view, before the State proclaimed it. Educationists might cry out for the need of culture for its own sake and for that of the individual. The workers of the country disregarded such a theory; employers of labour pooh-poohed the idea of education for all as worse than ridiculous, and loudly proclaimed that to use his tools should be the sum total of the workman's education.

But when nations compete with each other to supply the world's markets, they have to learn a great lesson : they must keep the pace. Twice in our century England, always distrustful of educational theories and theorists, has pulled up sharply, much as a driver who has mistaken the road in the dark. The first occasion was the International Exhibition of 1851, when it was evident that in artistic manufacture England had been receding for

International Exhibition, 1851.

some years, whilst Continental nations had pushed forward, and in certain cases left England behind. This was followed by the Exhibition of 1862, a revelation so shocking that it was the last of its kind in England. It is from the mid-century that the Technical Education movement more properly dates. To these Exhibitions we also partially owe our belated national system of education, rendered compulsory in 1876 and 1880. But the ten years of " book learning," between 1870 and 1880, did not produce the desired result. It would be perfectly safe to disregard the teaching of a Pestalozzi or a Froebel, who would educate the senses, for were they not theorists and therefore dispensable? But when Britain ploughed through a cycle of bad trade in the late seventies, when her markets were dull and closing, above all, when the great cry of " made in Germany " arose, even theories were able to obtain some attention. "We have too much education," sighed the Philistine ; an idea still quite common in England. "We have too little," rejoined those who well know that we may look strong on paper, and yet lack the essential. However it may be with the manufacturer, the schoolmaster is infinitely indebted to Germany for the inestimable service her growing exports have rendered his profession. His honour, dignity, even his pay have increased since it has been recognized that he has a great part to play in the production of national wealth. The need for better technical instruction has raked the educational ship from stem to stern. It begins with the worst kindergarten of the least favoured elementary school; it ends with the university.

It must not, however, be supposed that nothing had been done in the way of technical instruction until the State interfered. Almost invariably **Private Initiative.** this is one of the later stages to be reached in Britain; private initiative and local effort precede State intervention. In former days the ancient guilds and the system of apprenticeship undertook the instruction of those who would belong to an art or a craft.

A rapidly increasing population, the revolution effected in manufactures by steam as a motor power, and consequent massing of the workers in factories and works, required a different system of technical education. Through the great differentiation of labour in the more important industries, it was becoming, in some branches, increasingly difficult for a youth to pick up necessary knowledge by mere observation, and by rubbing shoulders with the older workers. Specialized instruction was fast becoming a necessity.

Naturally, it first made itself felt in the great centres of population. A Professor of Glasgow University, Dr. Geo. Birkbeck, filled with zeal for the education of the working classes, gave courses of lectures in that city on popular science subjects, following in the footsteps of Anderson and Black. The movement spread, Mechanics' Institutes arose all over Great Britain, and even reached the Colonies. Amongst the best-known of these is the Birkbeck Institution, founded in 1823, now carrying on its work in Chancery Lane, London, as actively to-day as when it was started, though now little used by the working classes. But the great ignorance of the workers in the early part of the century prevented such institutes reaping all the success which should have been theirs; those who wished to profit had frequently received no elementary education. Count Rumford, the first man who ever attempted to organize technical education, made the acquaintance of another serious difficulty: the professors were not sufficiently practical. Birmingham, always to the front in education and municipal activity, had a technical school in Bridge Street, and an excellent institute, long before Mason College was founded in 1875. Manchester and Bradford were not oblivious to the need of proper instruction. But, as M. Max Leclerc points out,[*] the first need was primary education. The Mechanics' Institutes dwindled into clubs; at least one could be

[*] *L'Éducation en Angleterre*, ch. 14.

named that became a music hall. The organization of elementary education, in 1870, led to a certain measure of technical instruction being given under the more progressive School Boards; the decks were finally cleared for action by the appointment of a Royal Commission, in 1881, to inquire into the matter.

The Report of 1884 shewed clearly that Britain, compared with other nations, was losing ground. In **Royal Commis-** particular, attention was drawn to the **sion on Technical** excellent technical schools existing in **Education, 1881.** Germany, to the thorough equipment of German leaders of industry. It was recognized that local needs must be considered, and that technical education, to be really fruitful, must follow a good general education. An Association for the Promotion of Technical Education, amongst its members Sir Hy. Roscoe, Mr. Arthur H. D. Acland (Vice-President of the Committee of Council, 1892–95), and the Secretary, Mr. Llewellyn Smith, worked to introduce a Bill to Parliament; and, finally, the Technical Instruction Act was passed in 1889, empowering local authorities to rate themselves to the extent of a penny in the £ (rateable value) for the advancement of technical instruction in elementary and secondary schools, and in local colleges and classes. In the year that followed, save in one or two of the better educated towns, the permission does not seem to have excited any enthusiasm: in Britain, education rates do not enjoy high popularity.

The following year, Mr. Goschen's budget shewed a considerable surplus, due to the increased beer and

Increased Beer and Spirit Duties, 1890. spirit duties levied for the purpose of compensating publicans whose licences were about to be extinguished. The temperance party made a great outcry that the Conservative Government wanted to use the nation's money for the purpose of rewarding their political allies, the publicans. Part of the sum, £300,000, was assigned to the Police Superannuation Fund, and the remainder, £743,000, was, on the motion of Mr. Arthur Acland, made applicable to technical education. Ever since, the sum has been continued, though it is sometimes rather smaller; an indication that British drinking habits are slightly decreasing.

The money thus wrested from the publican was divided amongst local authorities, County and Borough **County Councils and Technical Instruction.** Councils, and this gives us one more authority in education. Permission was granted either to use the money for the improvement of technical instruction or the diminution of the rates. Although the whole sum was not always used for educational purposes, yet Preston was the only borough which, up to the publication of the Report of the Royal Commission on Secondary Education (October, 1895), had used none at all. It had, however, granted a site for a technical school, and has since then consented to contribute £500 out of the extra Customs and Excise Duties. London* spent

---

* London does not always lead in matters educational. When the Act of 1870 was passed, it was enacted that School Boards should be elected, at the option of boroughs or districts. London was forthwith required to elect such Board.

nothing for the first two years, save a few hundred pounds on inquiries, out of an appropriation of £30,000. During the next three years £195,000 was expended altogether: for 1896-97 the Technical Education Board is estimating to spend £120,000; its entire appropriation is about £170,000.

The London Technical Education Board was formed in 1893. It consists of 35 members, representing the **London Technical Education Board, 1893.** L.C.C., the School Board, Trades' Council, and other bodies. Mr. Sidney Webb, L.C.C., is the chairman, and the Board secured the services of Dr. Wm. Garnett, the principal of the Durham College of Science, Newcastle-upon-Tyne, as secretary. It was decided to avoid all injurious competition with existing institutions, and to give the word "technical" as comprehensive a meaning as possible. Therefore the Board has aimed at assisting institutions of proved efficiency, or likely to become efficient with wise help. This is done by means of grants to build and furnish laboratories, science lecture halls, arts and crafts rooms; and by means of an admirable system of scholarships to enable children of elementary schools to pass into secondary schools, or continue their education in higher grade schools. Of the *Junior Scholarships*, **System of Scholarships.** 600 were offered in 1895-6, in the proportion of one girl to two boys. On inquiring the reason of this apportionment, the Secretary states that the demand on the part of the girls was very much smaller; but for this the Board itself would have favoured an equal division. The numbers for one half-yearly examination in May, 1895, boys and girls respectively, were :—

Entries, 1231 ... 853 ; passes, 651 ... 299 ; scholars, 225 ... 109

About 50 of these Junior Scholarships are open to children coming from secondary schools. A child's education is thus carried on for two years longer, from about 13 to 15 years of age.

Intermediate County Scholarships number 70, and give free education up to 18 or 19.

Senior County Scholarships are exhibitions at colleges of university rank. They are worth £60 per annum, and afford free education for three years

Besides these, the Board offers many scholarships for art, artistic handicrafts, technology, domestic economy ; these scholarships cover all kinds of technical work, and are for persons beyond school age desirous of self-improvement. It has close connection with the work of Polytechnics, Institutes, and other bodies, and has 65 different subjects, from plumbing to infant hygiene, taught or assisted by it in more than 700 separate classes and courses.

The Board comes into pretty close relationship with a large number of secondary schools, which it uses **Technical Board** for its scholarships. Practically such **and Secondary** schools are inspected by the Board, **Schools.** which judges if they are efficient in subjects within its scope, and helps them to become more so by grants. Though not exactly State intervention, such a work is allied to it, and, be it observed, it is sought by secondary schools which have in the past often loudly declaimed against outside interference. It hardly requires to be pointed out that the Technical Education Board uses the very means employed by the State itself to assume control of the elementary schools, means appealing to most practical teachers and governing bodies : a money grant depending on efficiency. Some of the old institutions, at work for many years in the technical field, *e.g.* the Birkbeck Institution, have been assisted to come into line with newer institutions, in order not to lose their pre-eminence by lack of proper equipment or teaching. Chemical students have been taught to correlate theoretical and laboratory work, which have too often been dissociated in the past. The Board lays great stress on practical work done in laboratories and workshops, thus implicitly condemning the knowledge of a science or craft derived merely from a text-book, divorced from practice and experiment. The Science and Art Department has ruled that no private or proprietary school which works for a profit to shareholders may be used by the Board for its scholarships and exhibitions. This ruling has not been strictly adhered to in the case of some girls' schools, and so far no case has been referred to the Local Government Board to test the legality of such payments.

Dr. Garnett reports that when the Board began its system of scholarships, in order to give any to girls at all, a lower standard had to be adopted than that of the boys ; at the very next examination, when the girls saw what was requisite, they pulled up, and answered to a similar standard.

The extension and development of the great Polytechnic Institutes deserves more than passing mention.

Polytechnics. Eleven of these people's colleges are now doing good work in London. Many of them, such as the Birkbeck Institution, the Regent Street Polytechnic, the People's Palace, the Borough Polytechnic, were at work long before the London Technical Education Board was created. Still, the "whiskey money" has enabled them to do more than ever before; in several cases, they have been entirely reorganized. Others, such as the Battersea, the South - Western (Chelsea), the Northern, and the Northampton Institute in Clerkenwell, are quite new, and have adopted the idea that they must study local needs. The class of persons using the Polytechnics depends very much on the neighbourhood. Woolwich, recently reformed on modern lines, and the Borough Polytechnic are almost entirely working class; Chelsea is supposed to be middle class; Battersea is lower middle and working class. Several of them have been founded and endowed by the Charity Commission, and work under its schemes.

A visit was paid to Battersea Polytechnic, because it happened to be close at hand, and because it has an important development in Domestic

Battersea Polytechnic, 1894. Economy. The building is imposing (red brick with stone dressings), with a respectable space in front, which too many London buildings lack. It still needs a great Assembly Hall to complete the original plan; yet, as it stands, it is a striking monument to the great revival in education amidst which we live. It would be difficult to ex-aggerate the impression conveyed to the mind by the great suites of workshops for carpenters, joiners, plumbers, bricklayers, masons, electrical engineers, blacksmiths, and other trades, all well attended in the evenings. There are admirable laboratories, lecture theatres, dark rooms for photographic processes; the Domestic Economy Department has space for laundry work, cooking, dressmaking; there are two admirable gymnasia for men and women, as well as a whole series of art class-rooms. The governing body had intended to dispense with the women's gymnasium as, though the Polytechnic cost about £45,000, funds were not too plentiful for so extensive a work. Fortunately the Charity Commissioners stepped in and provided the funds. Battersea Polytechnic is, moreover, conducting an experiment in co-education—a secondary day school for boys and girls; out of 116 pupils, 25 are girls. The course is much the same for both; but when the boys are at manual work, the girls take domestic economy. The principal, Mr. Sidney Wells, to whose organizing ability much of the success of the Poly-technic is due, states that up to July, 1896, there were 6500 class entries representing 2700 individuals, of whom 1042 (about two-fifths) were women. All classes are open to them, but naturally they do not attend certain trade classes.

The School of Domestic Economy, at Battersea, under Miss Corbold, is important, because not only are

Training School of Domestic Economy. students taught, but a certain number are trained to become teachers of the different subjects. The training extends over two years, embracing cookery, laundry work, dress cutting, hygiene, and housewifery. The London Technical Education Board offers valuable training scholarships in Domestic Economy, to be held at Battersea. The Technical Board estimated to spend £4200 on the teaching of Domestic Economy in 1896–97 in London. Very considerable grants are also given towards the provision of teaching in Science, Art, and Domestic Economy in girls' secondary schools, which, *mutatis mutandis*, are treated in precisely the same manner as the secondary schools for boys.

It scarcely needs to be said that the work of the London Technical Education Board is only a section of the technical instruction now being given throughout the country. Much of this work is new; according to its critics, some of it is crude; and it is more than probable that certain experiments will be abandoned or greatly modified. Yet it has seemed wiser, on the whole, to enter into a little fuller detail as to the work of one Board, in order to indicate its methods, and the possibilities that suggest themselves, rather than attempt to trace the work done all over the country, which, to be useful, would require, at the least, a volume to itself.

As already shewn, the Birkbeck Literary and Scientific

Institution has special claims to the gratitude of women,

The Birkbeck Literary and Scientific Institution. since it was the first educational institution to open its doors to them in the field of higher education. It began its career in 1823, when Dr. George Birkbeck, of Glasgow, founded it in Southampton Buildings. Its remarkable energy has permitted it to survive, and even to increase greatly in numbers and efficiency, although a host of similar institutions have arisen in or near London. At first the Birkbeck was a Mechanics' Institute, and so remained for many years; but to-day it would seem to be more used by the middle classes, although it is open to all. Though here classed under the heading of Technical Education, being assisted by the London Technical Education Board, and having a strong science side, the Birkbeck Institution is quite as strong in arts, having, out of a total of 4400 class entries, almost 1000 for the study of languages, besides many students in law, mental science, music, and a complete course of English subjects. A notable feature is the excellent preparation for London University Examinations. The Science and Technology subjects number twenty-eight, and are open to all without distinction of sex. The buildings, situated in Bream's Buildings, Chancery Lane, since 1885, are rather spacious and convenient than elegant. There is an important School of Art in the Institution, chemical and physical laboratories, reading-rooms used by both sexes, with an excellent lecture theatre. The principal is Mr. G. Armitage-Smith, M.A.

No description of technical instruction in England would be complete without some allusion to the work

City and Guilds of London Institute. undertaken by the City and Guilds of London Institute, although the share of women in the Institute is very small. It is significant that a small town like Zürich founded its École Polytechnique Fédérale in 1855; America its Massachusetts Institute of Technology in 1861; whereas London only began to think of its Technical College in 1876. The City and Guilds of London Institute is an association of the Livery Companies of London, founded in 1878; the offices of the Institute are at Gresham College, and its several branches of work are as follows:

(a) *The Central Technical College*, an imposing red brick building in Exhibition Road, Kensington, opened in 1884, provides education for those who already possess a sufficient knowledge of science or the arts to enable them to profit by instruction in the industrial applications of these. The college exists largely for the training of engineers, managers of works, responsible foremen, and technical chemists. The course lasts about three years. In December, 1896, there were over 200 students, of whom three were women.

(b) *The Technical College, Finsbury*, opened in 1883, is of a lower grade than the Central Technical College, and has an evening department for apprentices and others engaged during the day. There are almost 1100 day and evening students, about a dozen of whom are women attending the art department in the evening.

(*c*) In 1879 *The South London Technical Art School* was established by the Institute in Kennington Park Road. As its title implies, it is more concerned with decorative art than the other colleges of the trio.

The technological examinations, mostly held at 353 centres in the United Kingdom, form an important part of the work of the Institute. In 1895 there were about 25,000 students in attendance, in 739 classes throughout the kingdom; at the examinations, candidates worked more than 10,000 papers. The Institute attaches importance to manual training, and holds examinations in this subject also. The subjects of examination number more than sixty, and embrace soap manufacture, bread-making, electric lighting, goldsmiths' work, slate quarrying, dressmaking.

The Swedish system of manual training, known as Sloyd, in use at Herr Otto Salomon's seminary at Nääs,

Sloyd. Sweden, is only indirectly related to technical instruction, its aims being much wider. Sloyd is derived from a Swedish word meaning dexterous, and is related to the English sleight, in sleight of hand. But those who advocate Sloyd claim for it far more than the attainment of mere manual dexterity. The pupil gradually obtains higher mental powers by a series of steps in which hand, eye, brain, and judgment are equally exercised. Sloyd advocates claim that it is an important factor in the physical development of a child, over and above manual dexterity; it supplements gymnastics. Its mental and moral advantages are the cultivation of attention and interest,* the development of the powers of observation, of accuracy, practical common sense, perseverance, and patience.   It is clear therefore that the Sloyd system is not merely preparation for a trade, but a system graduated and developed on truly educational lines. It is specially suitable for boys and girls from about the age of eleven onwards.   Miss Chapman claimed a few years ago that a thousand Swedish national schools had adopted Sloyd.   In England it has not obtained so warm a reception, though many educationists are firm believers in its excellence.   A Sloyd Association of about 300 members works to spread the system. Classes may now be found in training colleges for teachers, as well as in schools of all grades.   In 1893 the Science and Art Department recognized Sloyd as a grant-earning subject, and it is expected to spread more rapidly in the future than has yet been the case.   Mr. T. G. Rooper, H.M. Inspector of Schools, alludes to Sloyd in these terms in the Blue Book of 1893 : " I hope that this valuable form of mental, moral, and manual discipline is taking firm root.   Of all the schools of manual training with which I am acquainted, I find Sloyd to be the most effective for developing delicacy of manipulation, thoroughness of workmanship, and truth in the senses of touch and sight."   At Nääs four courses of training for teachers, lasting six weeks each, are given every year ; advantage is taken of them by a considerable number of British students.

* See the paper read by Miss E. P. HUGHES, of Cambridge, at the College of Preceptors.   (W. Sotheran & Co., Petergate, York.)

Under the same roof as the Central Technical College, but not otherwise connected with it, is a **School of Art Wood Carving.** School of Art Wood Carving, under Miss Rowe as manager. Out of a total of 316 students in 1895, 256 were women, the remaining 60 being men. The latter are about equally divided as professional and amateur carvers, whereas about two-thirds of the women are amateurs. The remaining third, some eighty in all, are training as professional carvers, or as teachers of carving. Women have no great opening as carvers; they are not admitted to the trade workshops. Even if these were open, it is doubtful whether women's strength could stand the wear and tear the work necessitates. A man can work for nine or ten hours, whereas few women seem to be able to put in more than six, and of course this results in carving not being sufficiently remunerative to women. A few women have opened studios of their own; but here again the difficulty of getting good pay for good work besets them. Women, as one would expect, make excellent teachers of the subject, having sympathy with the difficulties of a learner, and a fair number obtain their training in this school. One of its main objects is to raise the old art of wood carving into the position it enjoyed in olden times, if possible. A yearly examination is held in which the student has to submit a certain number of carved examples; to carve a panel from a drawing or a photo in a given time; to be examined in scale drawing, *i.e.* drawing a chest or cupboard to scale;

to sketch a suitable carved decoration, and to answer a paper of technical questions.

The work of the Home Arts and Industries Association deserves brief mention, since out of about 4000 members of some 400 classes held all over the country, nearly a half are women; besides which, women are largely class-holders and teachers.   The Association was founded in 1884, and aims at the revival or teaching of the minor arts to the working classes, thus spreading a knowledge of artistic handiwork among the people.   Such arts are carpentry of various kinds, including inlay, *repoussé* work in brass and copper, bent iron, hand spinning and weaving, embroidery, sewing, pottery, leather work, wood carving, mosaic setting, basket making.   Teachers of these arts are voluntary or paid; in the latter case usually the class-holder is responsible for payment, either paying the teacher herself, or obtaining funds for the purpose, or charging a fee to members of the class.   Teachers are sometimes paid by grants from the County Council.   The work is very valuable for young persons who have left school and have spare time, especially for those in rural districts where amusements and educational facilities are scarce.   The Association may be said to work most successfully in small places, where the class-holder is enthusiastic and competent. A great improvement has been visible of recent years in the work produced, which may be seen at the annual exhibition of Home Arts and Industries held in June in the Royal Albert Hall.   Women do not solely take

Home Arts and Industries Association.

up the feminine industries named, such as weaving; they have been very successful in wood carving, basket-work, bookbinding, and other work.

Excellent technical instruction is given in the Man-chester Technical Schools; at Sheffield, in Firth College; at Newcastle; and, indeed, fairly good provision is found in most of the large towns, especially in Birmingham. But, of course, results are not equal all over the country. A considerable number of local (borough) authorities levy a rate for the purposes of the Technical Instruction Act; the borough of Preston at one time enjoyed the distinction of having the only Council which does not use the "whiskey money" for educational purposes.

On the other hand, it does not follow, because large sums are being spent upon technical instruction, **Share of Women** that women are greatly benefiting **in Technical** by such expenditure. Economically, **Instruction.** women are the poor sex, and they are poor for two reasons. Custom sanctions a lower wage for them than men, even when they are doing the same work equally well. But women who are properly qualified for their work suffer because other women are not competent, and because their sex is in a growing majority. So far as relief of the women's labour market is concerned, few things would produce a better result than recognition of the need of training and of specialization, of excellence in one department. On the other hand, there is no doubt that if a woman marries, a wider general knowledge, training in a course of domestic economy, is more valuable to her. Apart from considerations of culture, men find " multum, non multa" most advantageous; and so would women, if they had not to choose between the labour market and the prospect of marriage. For women who marry, " multa, non multum " is a far more suitable educational maxim.

Under these circumstances, it may be justifiable to ask whether women in the labour market will be materially **Domestic** benefited by the extension of domestic **Economy and** economy training to every girl. It **Bread-winning.** may be advisable, and even praiseworthy, for all to cook, sew, do laundry work and dressmaking ; but, unless there is a rise in the popularity of domestic service, one scarcely sees how a girl's place in the labour market will be affected. She has nothing to offer but what everyone else is offering.

The Women's Local Government Society has been at some trouble to conduct an inquiry as to how far **County Councils** women and girls share in the technical **and Women's** education provided by County and **Education.** Borough Councils. In a leaflet published by the Society in 1895, it appears that comparatively few Councils place women on their Technical Instruction Committees. In forty - nine cases, such Committees added persons other than Councillors to their numbers, but no women. Out of 124 County and Borough Councils, it is stated that only eighteen give equal educational advantages to the sexes. A few give nothing or next to nothing to girls ; the large majority give something, mostly domestic economy, nursing, dairy work. The inference of the Women's Local Government Society is that women should claim to sit on the local authorities, as the best method of safeguarding the interests of their sex. It is noteworthy that the technical education movement theoretically professes to embrace history, languages, literature ; but practically few Councils or Committees spare funds for the arts, even though they interpret the word "technical" as widely as possible. Now these subjects are usually more affected by women than men. Yet even if a greater expenditure were incurred for them in such subjects, it may be doubted whether their position in the labour market would be affected, or fresh employment be opened up to them. It would, however, contribute to a better general education of the sex. On the whole, even though Borough Councils remain closed to women, it must be admitted that they have scarcely succeeded in making their weight felt in this recent allocation of public money for educational purposes, or in expressing their wishes, supposing them to have any.

The Report of the Royal Commission on Secondary Education, 1894-95, lays great stress not only on the gaps in our educational system, but on the overlapping, the unnecessary competition it engenders, and on the need of organization. A survey of the field of Technical Education shows this clearly. The Science and Art Department is the central authority for Technical Education ; it is its *raison d'être*. The

Variety of Technical Instruction Authorities.

Education Department finds it necessary to have technical subjects in its newly-organized evening continuation schools; it sanctions and pays for quite a scheme of technical instruction for small girls in elementary day schools. There is scarcely a large town that has not some scheme of technical instruction to suit its local needs; for example, the Firth College at Sheffield, Mason College at Birmingham, Yorkshire College, Leeds, are successfully carried on by private or municipal enterprise, or both combined. It would be wrong to omit mention of School Boards, and their share in Technical Education; for though the Department is their central authority, not infrequently they assume the initiative, and only require its sanction for their work in higher grade schools. The University Extension movement, as is well known, must needs embrace technical subjects in its curriculum, else its usefulness would be greatly hindered. When during its career it throws off colleges like the University College at Nottingham, the Firth at Sheffield, or when it works them successfully as at Reading and Exeter, such subjects have to be well to the front. Nor does the Charity Commission disdain to meddle with technical instruction in its schemes for Secondary Education, since it is bound to consider a neighbourhood's needs. Frequently it has aided polytechnics, institutes, and schools by appropriating trust money to Technical Education. Lastly, we find the County Councils with a fresh power in their hands, the employment of funds for Technical Education.

The need for organizing and co-ordinating the work of so many and such various authorities scarcely requires mention. It is now recog-

Necessity for Organization. nized that before long every locality, borough, county, or district must needs have its own local educational authority; and a central authority must also be organized to co-ordinate the work of the Education Department, the Science and Art Department, and the Charity Commission, as well as to assume fresh powers over Secondary Education.

One of the most recent developments necessary to chronicle here is the opening of the London School of Economics and Political

London School of Economics and Political Science. Science in October, 1895. As is usual in educational matters, we lagged behind other countries in offering organized instruction in these subjects; on the other hand, notable progress has been made in a very short time. The Director, Mr. W. A. S. Hewins, reports that during the first year 300 students enrolled themselves in the School, of whom 100 took whole or part of the three years' course; seventy-five students were women. The School is already the largest centre of systematic training in its special subjects in the United Kingdom. The work is of University standard, and many of the students are graduates of British or foreign Universities. The lecture-list is large; for the Lent term of 1897 it covered such subjects as Geographical Conditions of the Seven Great Powers, Machinery of Administration in England, Problems of Trade Unionism, History of English Political Ideas during the Great Rebellion, Banking and Currency, Railway Economics and Statistics, Principles of Local Government, Local Taxation, Palæography and Diplomatics, and so forth.

An excellent Library of Political Science exists in connection with the London School of Economics, in Adelphi Terrace, Strand, which will eventually become very extensive. It is generously intended for the free use of persons engaged in public administration, national or municipal, and of all students of Economic or Political Science.

CONCLUSION

"THERE is now no such thing as a 'Woman's Education Question' apart from that of education generally," wrote Mrs. William Grey to Miss Buss in 1881. Her prophetic eye, cheered by the sight of many doors opening to her sex, foresaw the day when useless distinction shall no longer be drawn. An attempt has been made to shew briefly that though the day has dawned, it is not yet noon.

In Primary Education we see the great educational principle which forbids too early specialization, flung to the winds in the case of girls; we see a failure to attempt the cultivation of the powers of observation, in that drawing is not compulsory for them. In Secondary Education it is difficult to generalize, for the variety of schools is very great, and usually those who know about boys' schools do not know about girls'.

It is probably true that the best girls' schools are equal to the best boys' schools; indeed, some authorities are heard to declare that the former are superior. Yet here it must be remembered that girls' first-class schools are fewer in number than good boys' schools. In Technical Education, which the Royal Commission of 1894–95 declared to be a branch of Secondary Education, women have not obtained a fair share of the opportunities afforded, probably because they have not clearly indicated their wants.

Turning to Higher Education, we find a wide discrepancy between the numbers of men and women students. The sexes are represented at Oxford and Cambridge as 6000 to 400 in round numbers. The opening of more employments to women, and higher rewards for their labour, are of prime necessity as direct incentives to women's education. A woman can no more, indeed rather less, afford to throw away an expensive training than can a man. Some substantial advantage must lie at the end of it. A fair number of women have now received an excellent training in natural science, holding the B.Sc. of Cambridge or London. Hardly any employment is open to such women save that of science mistress, with the modest salary of £100. Attention has been drawn to the fact that occasionally, as in the appointment of head teachers of art schools, the best posts are still closed to women in certain branches. This is not entirely due to masculine selfishness; public opinion and custom are also factors. Women are largely shut out of administration, which, according to many high authorities, Ruskin amongst them, is their great talent. Scarcely anything is given to them in the Education Department, including South Kensington. The exceptions have been noted in their place. Women are shut out of almost all the medical

schools in the provinces.   Great as is the progress that
has been made, many things yet remain to be done.

I have endeavoured to avoid the implication or
suggestion that the education of women is, at bottom,
a sex question.   So far is it from being a blow aimed
by women at the supremacy of the privileged sex, that
the movement has really been begun by men.   From
Comenius and Erasmus downwards, a section of educated men have struggled for the acknowledgment of
women's claim to education as many of them have
never dreamt of doing.   Without the loyal and generous
aid that men have given, nothing could have been done.
In many cases it was not help that was rendered : it was
even the initiation of a reform.   To those who have
followed the movement for women's education, mention
of how the matter really stands is about as necessary
as to allude to the fact that Queen Anne is dead.

Yet whilst sex is not the true dividing line on this,
or indeed on most other matters, it is useless to shut
our eyes to the fact that men of a certain stamp, not
usually themselves intellectual, are jealous of women's
attainments, and assume a discouraging attitude.
Similarly, a large number of women find that ignorance, real or pretended, is a recommendation.   It is
difficult to think of any wider cause of the low level
of general culture than this, though it has obviously
lessened with the march of the century.

So far as I have been able to discover, women's
education makes the most sure advance where women
officer largely or entirely the educational institutions

which have been called into existence, where they sit upon the committee of management, and take a large share of the teaching. The reason of this appears to be that girls are more encouraged by what women can do than by what men have done. It would be invidious to point to institutions which have failed to keep pace with the times because the necessity of giving women a large share of the work has not been grasped; but it would be possible to do so. So great is the hopefulness of the women engaged in the education of their sex, so powerful is their example to stimulate those under their care, so able are they to deal with the various difficulties that arise, that the success of the movement seems only assured when it remains largely in women's own hands. It is sometimes said, and with a certain amount of truth, that the great advance in education has called forth a new type of woman, strong, just, capable. Probably the type was never lost; it existed far back in our history. But for the last two or three hundred years, opportunities for exercising women's abilities have been lacking. Where the home did not absorb them, energy and capacity must have been largely wasted.

In speaking with men and women of other nations, and comparing some of the points of difference in educational methods, more than one educationist has observed to me: "Our system looks well on paper." Now this is what the English system, if the expression may be permitted, does not do. No attempt has here been made to conceal its anomalies, insufficiency, inefficiency, its weakness, the narrowness of the area marked by real excellence. Yet to those who can interpret the signs, it is certain that something great will work itself out, and is even now in the casting. It was said of Louis XIV. by a judge of character: " Il se mettra tard en route, mais il y arrivera "; and this forecast will be true of English education. For we shall profit by the mistakes that other nations have committed, making haste slowly; above all, we shall aim at conserving the genius of the Anglo-Saxon race, its individuality, self-reliance, power to assume the initiative.

It is characteristic of the English people to be highly critical of themselves and their performances. We laud the educational systems of France and Germany, largely because we do not know them. And yet France, who is far from being blind to our national peculiarities, sends over M. Max Leclerc to inquire how men are made in England. His mission is thus summed up by M. Emil Boutmy, in the preface of the book he has written :* "Where on the other side of the Channel are the upper and middle classes educated and formed from which political life draws its parliamentary repre-sentatives and diplomats, the administration its officials, the army and navy their officers, industry its leaders, commerce its merchants, philosophy such profound thinkers, literature, history, science, such original talent ? What means of preparation have been at the disposal of this *élite*, whom we meet in all the quarters of the

* *L'Éducation en Angleterre.* By MAX LECLERC ; preface by EMIL BOUTMY. Armand Colin et Cie., Paris.

globe, ever ready, never lacking, adapted to every variety of the work awaiting them, indefatigable builders of the national greatness? What do these men owe to the family, to public spirit, to the school and their masters? What have the State and legislation done for them?"

M. Max Leclerc has a good deal to say about the insufficiency, incoherence, and lack of adaptation in English education; but he has also somewhat to say touching our physical energy, moral force, individuality left uncramped by a uniform artificial type, our saving idea that education does not end with school life. We shall do well to note not only the faults, but the excellencies of English education, in order that the wheat may not be pulled up with the tares.

If this attempt to report progress in women's education had been written fifty years ago, the task would have been a very brief one. The Birkbeck Institution had opened its doors to women. The Governesses' Benevolent Institution had begun to think that poverty and incompetence were not unconnected. In fifty more years will women have travelled as fast and as far? The answer is doubtful; but it is safe to prophesy that before then the barriers will have been all thrown down. The tools will be for him, and even for her, who can use them.

PART II.

EDUCATION IN SCOTLAND

PART II. has been kindly contributed to this little
volume—

PRIMARY AND SECONDARY EDUCATION
  By Mr. G. W. ALEXANDER, Clerk to the School
  Board of Glasgow.

HIGHER AND TECHNICO-PROFESSIONAL EDUCATION
  By Miss JANE GALLOWAY, Hon. Sec. to Queen
  Margaret College, Glasgow.

PART II.

EDUCATION IN SCOTLAND

Section I.

Primary Education

IN Scotland, as in England, education in its beginnings is associated with the monasteries. Their schools were intended primarily for the training of those who meant to devote themselves to the service of the Church, but in time they came to be taken advantage of by the upper classes. As the demand for education increased, the monks instituted schools in the towns adjoining the monasteries, and in these the Burgh or High schools of Scotland appear to have had their origin. Frequently also schools seem to have been carried on in connection with the country churches, and many of these were gifted to the monasteries, and so came under their supervision. In this way it became true that "before the Reformation it was the monk, and not the parish priest, who held the ecclesiastical power, and played the chief part in the history of education."*

* *History of Early Scottish Education.* By J. EDGAR, M.A.

It is generally supposed that education in Scotland prior to the Reformation is scarcely worthy of notice; but Mr. Grant, in his *History of Burgh Schools*, and Mr. Edgar show that the early records prove the existence long before the Reformation of four kinds of schools : (1) Parish schools, under the instruction or supervision of the parish priest; (2) Cathedral schools ; (3) Collegiate schools, connected with churches having a college or chapter ; and (4) Sang schools, of which the primary function was music. There can be little doubt that John Knox, instead of requiring to break fresh ground, had already a substantial basis for the system he sought to establish. Indeed, as early as 1494, when James IV. was king, we have provision made for the compulsory attendance of certain classes, a statute being passed which required all barons and freeholders of substance to send their eldest sons to school from the age of six or nine until "they be competentlie founded and have perfite Latine." The penalty for disobedience was twenty pounds. No special provision appears to have been made for girls, but there is evidence that at all events the daughters of the wealthier classes shared in such education as was considered essential at the time.

Pre-Reformation Schools.

The Reformation, while it appears to have robbed education of the endowments it enjoyed through its connection with the Church, gave a great impetus to the establishing of a national system. *The First Book of*

Landowners and Education.

Discipline, published by the Reformed Church in 1560, provided for a school in every parish and town, as well as "colleges" in the "notable" towns. The General Assembly of the Church did what it could to carry out this scheme, but it had no power to levy assessments; and although in 1616 the Privy Council passed a decree obliging each parish to maintain a school and school-master, the decree was not confirmed by Parliament till 1633. The subsequent political turmoil stood in the way of educational advancement; it was not till after the Revolution that the State succeeded in making general provision for the instruction of the people, and placed education in a position to secure its regular development. In 1696 an Act was passed which laid upon the heritors or landowners of every parish the duty of providing a school and appointing a schoolmaster. The salary was not to be less than 100 merks (£5 11s. 1½d.), nor more than 200 merks (£11 2s. 2⅔d.). The Presbyteries had power to compel the heritors to carry out the Act, and they were also entrusted with the superintendence of the schools so established. This right of superintendence of the parish schools remained with the Presbyteries until 1872, though it was slightly modified in 1861.

For more than one hundred years after 1696, the State did nothing further for education in Scotland. At the beginning of the present century the progress of the nation made fresh provision absolutely necessary. In 1803 an Act was passed by which a school-house was to be provided in every parish where none already

existed; and in large or populous parishes additional
schools, generally known as side schools, were to be
supplied. The salary of the schoolmaster was raised
to not less than 300 nor more than 400 merks, and
was to be fixed by the heritors and minister. To
this were added a free house and garden and school
fees. The latter were also fixed by the heritors and
minister, and the schoolmaster was obliged to teach
such poor children as they recommended. "The
schoolmaster's house and plot of garden ground was a
feature of each Scotch parish, along with the minister's
manse and glebe; and, like the minister, the teacher
was a freeholder. The parish school was, in short,
an adjunct of the parish church. The teacher was
examined and approved by the Presbytery. The
minister was an elector along with the heritors. To
him the general superintendence of the school was
assigned. And, lastly, the teacher was required to
subscribe the Confession of Faith and the formula
of the Church of Scotland."* This description, with
modifications as to salaries and religious tests to be
noted later, held true till 1872.

One part of the country—the Highlands and Islands
—had, however, lagged behind; and in 1838 it was
Special Provision found necessary to authorize the
for the Commissioners of the Treasury to
Highlands. provide and endow schools in High-
land parishes, and these came to be known as "Par-

---

* *The State in its Relation to Education.* By HENRY CRAIK, C.B.

liamentary" schools, to distinguish them from "Parish" and "Side" schools. Five years later, however, in 1843, occurred the ecclesiastical crisis which resulted in what is known as the Disruption of the Established Church of Scotland and the foundation of the Free Church, and this had an important effect on education. So far as they could, the Free Church opened schools in connection with their churches, and the accommodation and facilities for education were thereby largely increased. The effect was seen in the Act of 1861, which, after raising salaries to a minimum of £35 and a maximum of £70, transferred the examination of parochial schoolmasters from the Presbyteries to the Universities, abolished the religious test in the case of burgh schoolmasters, and modified it for parochial schoolmasters to a declaration that they would not teach opinions opposed to the Bible or Shorter Catechism, or exercise the functions of their office to the prejudice of the Established Church.

But this Act of 1861 is particularly interesting, as it appears to contain the first official recognition of the education of girls. Hitherto boys

Appointment of Women Teachers. and girls had been taught side by side in the parish schools, and, as a rule, the curriculum for both was the same. This Act, however, gave the heritors and minister power to appoint a "female teacher . . . to give instruction in such branches of female industry and household training, as well as of elementary education, as they shall then or from time to time prescribe, and to provide . . . a yearly sum not exceeding thirty pounds as a salary for such female teacher."

A report obtained in 1838 had shown that out of 4000 teachers included in the returns only 700 were women, and these were all either conducting schools of their own, or employed in privately endowed schools. How little things had changed in 1861 is seen from the Blue-book for that year, which, referring to the small number of women teachers in Scotland, says, "It is urged, by way of explanation, that the employment of female teachers in separate departments of schools for the poor is comparatively new in Scotland, and cannot be expected to make rapid way. This argument concedes that the establishment of training schools for females in Scotland has been at least in some degree excessive or premature." To appreciate this last remark fully, it must be remembered that Government had already been paying grants for training schoolmistresses in Scotland for *twelve* years. At this time only twenty - five per cent. of all the teachers employed (other than pupil teachers) were women, and of the pupil teachers 30·4 per cent. In 1872, the last year of the old *régime*, the percentages were 33·5 and 41·8 respectively; in 1896 they were 61·6 and 80·6.

As in England, pupil teachers had come to be freely employed; in 1861 they formed 62 per cent. of the total teaching staff. This resulted from the special inducements offered by the Government in the shape of grants. In the matter of training teachers,

Scotland was well in advance, for already, in 1826, David Stow had instituted his Normal system; the first special building had been opened in 1837, to be followed by three others before 1846, when grants began to be regularly given.

Scotland shared with England the grants assigned to education from 1833 onwards, and, generally speaking, on the same terms, though by 1860 special stress was being laid on instruction in sewing and cutting out in schools where girls were taught, and it was made a condition of the grant. Inspection, however, was optional, and only schools which desired a grant were subject to it. Many of the parochial schools preferred to dispense with the grant, and were satisfied with the annual visitation of the Presbytery. In most cases this was a useful function; in others, the visitors simply sat by while the schoolmaster examined his classes on lessons which had been specially prepared for at least a week previously. By this method the report seldom failed to be satisfactory.

Government Grant, 1833.

The want of inspection, however, did not necessarily imply any want of efficiency in the instruction. The teacher was, in most cases, under the supervision of the minister of the church with which his school was connected; and, as a public functionary, he was also under the supervision of the community, especially in country districts. Further, the multiplication of schools due to ecclesiastical

Efficiency of Scottish Teachers.

differences secured even for the village schoolmaster the stimulus of competition, for the school fees formed, as a rule, the largest part of his income ; and most parents chose a school for their children irrespective of their denominational views.   It is to be remembered too that the parish schoolmaster had had, as a rule, a more or less complete university education, and in many instances held a licence as a clergyman.   Even in the country parishes his scholarship was not allowed to rust.   All classes sent their children to the parish school, and usually there were one or two lads looking forward to the University.   It has been alleged, and in many cases no doubt with truth, that the schoolmaster devoted too much of his attention to the most advanced pupils, and neglected the rest of the school ; but at least it deserves mention that in not a few cases preparation for the University was given before and after the ordinary school hours without extra fee or reward.   Perhaps no better testimony to the quality of schools in Scotland at this time can be found than the fact that not a little of the famous Revised Code had to be abandoned so far as Scotch schools were concerned.   It is not to be supposed, however, that the parish schools, valuable as they were, possessed any monopoly of education.   Just as they contributed to secondary education in the country, so the grammar schools in the town contributed to elementary education. Not only were scholars admitted to these at an early age, but it sometimes occurred that one school served as burgh and parish school combined.   Generally speaking, however, the burgh schools had more of a secondary character. They will be more conveniently dealt with under the heading of Secondary Education.

In addition to the parish and burgh schools, there were spread over the country a large number of private and endowed schools. In **Private and Endowed Schools.** 1837 there would appear to have been 3354 non-parochial, as against 1053 parochial schools. In 2329 of the former which sent in returns, there were 73,867 boys and 54,451 girls, as compared with 39,604 boys and 22,317 girls in 924 parochial schools. Of the non-parochial schools 753 had some form of endowment, while 1318 were supported entirely by the school fees. The endowments were divided pretty fairly between boys and girls. The Endowed Schools Commissioners of a later date were of opinion that in respect of endowments girls had not been neglected. Even of the private schools the majority were mixed. Some were, however, for girls only ; and as needlework came to be taught, a few so-called Female Industrial schools were established, which, however, had nothing in common with Industrial schools as we now know them.

The fees seemed to have varied in the parish schools from 1*d.* to 6*d.* a week, with extra charges of from 2*d.* to 6*d.* for higher branches. In the other schools there was no uniformity, and schools might be found with any scale of charges.

The Act of 1861 must have given a considerable

impetus to education, for we find in 1867 that out

Impetus afforded by the Act of 1861. of 500,000 children some 400,000 were at school; though only about the half of this number were at schools under inspection.

Such numbers, at a time when education was neither free nor compulsory, prove how general was the appreciation of education, and how real what has so often been called the spirit of education in Scotland.

The consequence was that when further legislation became necessary, it was possible to make that legislation at once more complete and less complicated than in England. The people were in favour of increased educational facilities. The landowners had been taxed for the support of schools for nearly two hundred years, and consequently the principle of assessment did not require to be introduced, but only extended. Class distinctions had not been strongly marked in educational arrangements, and generally the question was less one of establishing a new system than of bringing the existing system into line with modern opinion.

The distinction between the Acts for England and Scotland appears in the very titles. The former is "The Elementary Education Act, 1870—an Act to provide for Public Elementary Education in England and Wales"; while the latter is "The Education (Scotland) Act, 1872—an Act to amend and extend the Provisions of the Law of Scotland on the subject of Education."

Differences between the Scottish and English Systems. The English Act has been so well summarized in the part of this work dealing with England that the Scotch system may best be described in contrast with it.

1. While the English Act left it to the towns and parishes to decide whether there should be a School Board or not, so long at all events as the necessary accommodation was voluntarily supplied, the Scotch **Election of School Boards obligatory.** Act made the election of a School Board obligatory on every burgh and parish within twelve months after the passing of the Act. The number of members varies from five to fifteen, according to population, and women are eligible for membership. The method of voting is cumulative, and elections take place every three years. In Scotland the elections of all School Boards take place about the same time, while in England the different dates of forming School Boards make anything like uniformity in time of election utterly impossible.

2. While in England localities were at first left free to decide whether school attendance should be compulsory or not, and a compulsory **Compulsory Attendance, 1872.** system only became general in 1880; in Scotland attendance became universally compulsory in 1872. The English system of bye-laws by which each locality can, subject to the Education Department, fix its own standard of exemption, was not adopted in Scotland. The Scotch

Education Department, under the powers given them by the Act, fixed the fifth standard as the exemption standard for the whole country. This may appear lower than in some parts of England; but it is to be remembered that the half-time system, with its still lower exemption standard, has never prevailed in Scotland to the same extent, even in proportion to the population, as in England.

It might have been supposed that from the important position education had so long held in Scotland, a less stringent compulsory system would have sufficed. It is, however, a curious fact that the penalties for non-attendance at school in Scotland are much heavier than in England, the maximum penalty being in the latter country 5s. including expenses, and in the former 20s. in addition to expenses up to a second sum of 20s., with imprisonment in default of payment.

From time to time the raising of the exemption standard from the fifth to the sixth has been suggested. The Department, however, have not been convinced of the advantages of such a step, and preferring to work by attraction rather than by further compulsion, they some years ago instituted a "Merit Certificate" for scholars over thirteen years of age. The certificate requires thorough efficiency in the three elementary subjects, two class subjects, and all the stages of one specific subject or two stages of two specific subjects other than domestic economy. The teacher must certify to the character and conduct of each pupil admitted to the examination which forms part of the

annual inspection of each school presenting candidates.
During the last four years 8603 of these certificates have
been issued.

3. A School Board in England might find the supervision of school attendance its principal work, and
might not have a single school under
its management. The transference
of schools is entirely optional. In
Scotland, on the contrary, the burgh and parish schools
and all other schools established under previous Acts
of Parliament were at once transferred to the Boards,
which received the powers and obligations of the heritors
and minister, the authority of the Presbyteries being likewise abolished so far as concerned public schools.

Fuller Powers of Scottish Boards.

Only seven Boards in Scotland have no schools, and
this is owing to their districts being supplied by the
schools of an adjoining Board, generally a burgh Board
in the same parish.

The School Boards were authorised to accept transference of other schools, and within a few years
practically all the State-aided schools in Scotland, with
the exception of those connected with the Roman
Catholic and Episcopalian Churches and the Practising
Schools of the Training Colleges, were under the
Boards. Even private schools have been absorbed in
considerable numbers.

4. While in England the grants were confined mainly
to elementary education, and are not paid beyond the
seventh standard, the limit in Scotland is one of age,
namely 18; and this, combined with the management

R

of burgh or grammar schools, gives the Scotch Boards

School Boards and Secondary Education. wide powers in providing secondary as well as elementary instruction. The Act of 1872 specially provided that "the standard of education which now exists in the public schools shall not be lowered."

5. In Scotland School Boards are left free to make any provision they choose for religious instruction before

The Shorter Catechism. or after the hours set apart for secular instruction, subject only to the ordinary conscience clause. There is no prohibition of religious Catechisms or formularies distinctive of particular denominations, as in England. The Bible and the Shorter Catechism are commonly taught according to what had been "use and wont" before the passing of the Act, although some Boards have now discontinued the Catechism.

6. The Scotch Education Department, like the English, have at their disposal a limited number of pensions

Teachers' Pensions. for teachers; but in addition, power is given to School Boards to grant teachers such retiring allowances as they think fit. This also was not a new principle in the Scotch education system, for the parochial teachers who held office *ad vitam aut culpam* were legally entitled to a pension, and their rights were specially reserved by the Act of 1872.

Free Education, 1889. Education in Scotland began to be made free in 1889, when Parliament voted a sum in relief of fees to be distributed under conditions framed by the Scotch Education Department. Subsequent Acts readjusted and increased the amounts available, but they did not interfere with the Department's power to make conditions. No fees can be charged now to scholars between the ages of three and fifteen; but in the larger towns where there is sufficient accommodation for all children who desire free education, the School Boards have been allowed to carry on a small number of fee-paying schools.

Numbers of Scholars in the Schools. The following statistics, taken from the latest Blue-book, show the number of children on the rolls, &c., and the number enjoying free education :—

Estimated total number of children of school age (five to fourteen) 867,062

Number on rolls of schools on annual grant list . . 708,551

Number on rolls of schools actually inspected last year 692,202*

* Of these 661,971 were of school age (5–14), 12,820 were between three and five years of age, and 17,410 were beyond fourteen.

Number present at inspection—

Boys	331,235
Girls	313,775
	645,010

Number in average attendance in schools inspected :

	Boys.		Girls.	
Public Schools . .	258,065	...	234,875	
Established Church Schools .	2,934	...	3,089	
Free Church Schools .	1,986	...	2,180	
Episcopal Schools . .	5,756	...	5,749	
Roman Catholic Schools .	24,353	...	23,008	
Undenominational and other Schools . . .	6,446	...	6,864	
	299,540	...	275,765	575,305

Number of scholars in free schools . . 672,093, or 97·09 %

Number of scholars in fee-paying schools . 20,109, or 2·91 %

Accommodation is now provided for 789,126 scholars, as compared with 281,688 in 1872.

Scotland has not so far followed England in the matter of inspection of the day schools. The annual inspection stills holds its place, but it is of a general character, except in the fifth or exemption standard, which is examined individually, as are also pupils presented in specific subjects.

Perhaps nothing in the history of Scottish education is more noteworthy than the increased recognition of the special requirements of girls. It **Special Subjects for Girls.** is true that the schools, excepting some of the High schools and Voluntary schools, continue to be "mixed" and to include children of all ages, from infants upwards. It is true also that, generally speaking, the curriculum for boys and girls is the same as far as the ordinary branches are concerned, and on this account there is much greater difficulty in arranging for special subjects than when girls are taught by themselves in separate departments. Needlework, however, has been made obligatory, and special inducements in the way of grants are held out for teaching cookery, laundry work, and dairy work, as well as general domestic economy and hygiene. Such instruction is always of a practical nature ; and though laundries are still, as a rule, confined to schools in larger towns, well equipped cookery rooms are now fairly general. Drawing, which is not compulsory even for boys in Scotland, is now being taught in an increasing number of schools to both sexes. Until quite recently the physical training of girls was an optional matter, and probably received little attention beyond the calisthenics of the infant room. Now, however, some form of drill or physical exercise must be taught to all scholars if the higher grant for organization and discipline would be earned. In some of the larger towns swimming is taught to the older girls who desire it.

It is obvious that with even one or two special subjects the girls are overweighted as compared with the boys; but the Code now offers inducements to teachers to give instruction in elementary science to boys while the girls are at needlework, and the latter are understood to be judged more leniently in arithmetic. It is a question, however, whether girls would not derive greater benefit from a shorter course of arithmetic thoroughly mastered than from the longer course imperfectly understood.

As already shown, the greater part of the teaching in Scotland in now done by women. As the mixed schools, except small country schools, are usually under head-masters, and separate departments for **The Training of** girls and infants are rare in Scotland **Elementary** as compared with England, the **Teachers.** opportunities for women becoming head-mistresses are few. They may have obtained their certificates in the ordinary way through a training college, or they may have served as pupil teachers and then qualified themselves by teaching and examination, without attending a training college, or they may have obtained one of the university titles or certificates; the woman over eighteen years of age approved by the Inspector is almost unknown in Scotland, and ranks only as a pupil teacher.

While the number of men seeking admission to the training colleges is at present decreasing, the number of women not only willing, but by examination eligible to be trained is largely in excess of the number the colleges are authorized to admit.

Since the lectures and degrees of the Scottish Universities were opened to women, the privilege of attending university classes, hitherto confined to the men, has been extended to the most distinguished women students of the training colleges. It is to be noted that the Scotch training colleges are all nominally denominational, though in practice students of all churches are found in them.

The Code for 1895 contained provisions for the training of teachers in connection with the universities, but the conditions attached will probably prevent any great accession to the ranks of teachers by this avenue.

The latest returns show that the schools are staffed by

8907 certificated teachers, of whom 4871 are women;

2027 assistant teachers, of whom 1866 are women;

4268 pupil teachers, of whom 3297 are girls and 179 "women over 18."

The average salary is—

			Principals			Assistants		
Masters	.	.	.	£169	5	4 ...	£100	16	11
Mistresses	.	.	,	£76	1	8 ...	£64	2	8

Certificated teachers count for 70 pupils, assistant teachers for 50, except those who have passed third class in the Queen's Scholarship examination, who count for 40, and pupil teachers for 25.

The Department have abolished the annual examination of pupil teachers, and now hold one examination at the end of the second year of apprenticeship. Those who fail in this examination, unless from illness or other sufficient cause, do not continue the work. Certain leaving certificates, however, exempt candidates from this examination.

Evening schools have made rapid progress in Scotland during the last twenty-four years, but more particularly **Evening** since 1893, when the special Code for **Continuation** Evening Continuation Schools was **Schools.** first issued. Formerly the classification was by standards, as in the day schools, and individual examination prevailed. Now, however, the grants are paid on the average attendance of all pupils over twelve years of age, and on the quality of the instruction as tested by visits without notice. In 1872 the average attendance at inspected evening schools in Scotland was 3653, of whom 1236 were girls. In 1892–93, the last session under the old regulations, the average attendance was 19,575, of whom 4894 were girls. In the last session (1895–96) the average attendance had increased to 45,487, of whom scarcely a third were girls.

As, except in one or two details, the Codes for England and Scotland are alike, the evening schools are worked on much the same lines as in England, and full advantage has been taken of the opportunity to institute classes in subjects specially suited for women and girls, such as domestic economy, health and hygiene, cookery, laundry work, and dressmaking. An increasing number of girls is also to be found taking such subjects as book-keeping, shorthand, and typewriting. As a rule the instruction in the evening schools is given by the day school teachers.

The cost of education is met in the same way as in England, partly from the Imperial Treasury, partly from local sources. In 1894–95 the amount of Parliamentary grant paid to day schools was £614,000, or £1 1s. 4¼d. for each scholar in average attendance; the amount paid in relief of fees at 12s. per head was £349,000, of which £302,000 was paid to School Boards and £47,000 to managers of Voluntary schools. Local sources contributed in the shape of rates £702,000, an average rate of 8·18 pence, Voluntary subscriptions £31,000, and school fees £25,000.*

Cost of Education.

The cost of "maintenance" per child in average attendance was, in public schools £2 9s. 2¾d., and in Voluntary schools £2 3s. 4½d., of which last amount 7s. 3¼d. was met by subscriptions and 2s. 8½d. by fees.

---

* Ciphers have been substituted for the three last figures.

SECTION II.

Secondarp Education

IN Scotland education has so long been generally
regarded as a whole that it is somewhat difficult to
draw a clear line of distinction between primary and
secondary education. Certainly there have always been
two kinds of public schools—the parish and the burgh
schools—but it is open to doubt whether the difference
between them did not lie less in the education given
than in the social status of the scholars, for the higher
fees of the burgh schools naturally confined them to
children of a wealthier class than attended the parish
schools.

So far as public education of a higher character had
a visible existence it was in the burgh schools, and
it may be well briefly to trace their
The Burgh Schools. history. As already stated, these
schools had their origin in schools
founded by the monks in the towns surrounding the
monasteries. In course of time the Town Councils
came to have an interest in the management, seemingly
by contributions to their support. Even before the
Reformation we find some Town Councils asserting their

right to appoint masters independently of the Church
authorities. "The master of the schools was in some
instances endowed from Church lands; but in the
great majority of cases he was paid from the common
good of the burgh or by voluntary assessments imposed
by the burgesses for his behoof, and by the fees and
other perquisites payable by scholars."* The buildings
appear to have been erected and repaired at the expense
of the burghs.

At the time of the Reformation John Knox's scheme
included a full provision of higher schools, intermediate
between the primary schools and the
John Knox's Scheme. universities, and he and his colleagues
made great efforts to retain part of
the Church endowments for education. In this, however, they met with but little success; and, except in
the larger towns, the gap between the primary schools
and the universities had to be bridged over by the
parish schools extending their curricula beyond primary
limits, while the universities met these schools by junior
classes, which would have been unnecessary had the
original plan of the Reformers been carried out.
Though, however, the Church failed so far, it did not
cease to take an active interest in the grammar schools
that were established, and the jurisdiction of Presbyteries over the burgh schools was only occasionally
questioned until in 1861 it was at once indisputably
confirmed by a decision of the Court of Session,
and then finally abolished by the Schoolmasters' Act

* *History of the Burgh Schools of Scotland.* By JAMES GRANT, M.A.

of that year. As a rule the Town Councils were the managers; but in cases where one school served both as a burgh and parish school the Town Councils and heritors acted jointly.

The curriculum in the earliest days was, as may be supposed, entirely classical, Latin receiving special attention, and Hebrew being not un-

Curriculum of a Burgh School. known. It was assumed that scholars entering the grammar schools had already learned to read and write; but as time went on it was found advisable to add English and writing to the curriculum. Arithmetic and mathematics do not find a regular place till towards the close of the seventeenth century. The only modern language taught before recent days was French, which no doubt owed its place in the curriculum to the close association between Scotland and France in former times. As might be expected, both from the origin of the schools and the interest taken in them by the Reformers and their successors, religious instruction formed a very important part of the teaching, but parents were entitled to withdraw their children from it if they chose. In the Sang schools music was second only to Latin; but for some reason, after the Reformation, it gradually decayed in spite of special legislation, and in certain cases, special endowments.

The schools were maintained after the Reformation

How the Burgh Schools were maintained. by a payment from the common good or common property of the burgh, by the school fees, and in some cases

by endowments.   The principal part of the masters'
salaries was the fees, which were separate for each
subject, and generally each master received the fees
for his own classes.   Naturally each endeavoured to
secure as many pupils as possible for his own subject,
and the result was frequently keen rivalry between the
masters of the same school.   As a rule, each was head
of his own department, so that a grammar school was
rather a collection of schools for separate subjects.
The rector was nominally head, but he had limited
powers beyond his own department, which was usually
that of classics.   In 1868 the annual average fee per
scholar seems to have ranged from 6s. 2d. to £10 3s.;
but few fell below £1.   At one time the masters also
received certain perquisites, not the least curious of
which were dues for an annual bout of cockfighting,
to which the school was given up on Shrove Tuesday
or Fasterns' E'en.

About the middle of the last century a demand appears
to have arisen for a curriculum in which commercial
and science subjects, and not classics,
**Rise of
"Academies."** should hold the principal place.   The
result was the establishment of a
number of "Academies," erected mainly by public
subscription.   According to Mr. Grant, "though at
first the academies were intended merely to supplement
the grammar schools, in a short time they superseded
or absorbed them; and in a few instances, instead of
amalgamating with them, became their rivals."   In some
cases the Town Councils alone managed these schools;

but generally the governing body was composed of
representatives of the subscribers and Town Councils,
and certain persons *ex officiis.*

In addition to the burgh schools and academies,
there was also a considerable number of endowed
schools which contributed to the
Endowed and higher education of the country.
Private Schools.
Many of these were carried on as
what used to be known as " Hospitals," that is to say,
the pupils were not only educated but also boarded
and clothed. The last Endowments Commission
abolished this system, and converted the former
hospitals into day schools, with a large number of
bursaries attached to them.

There was also, of course, a large number of private
and proprietary schools in which advanced instruction
was given, and which were attended mainly by the
children of the wealthier classes.

Secondary Education in Scotland has owed something
also to endowments which were not confined to a
particular school, but were of a more general character.
The Commission of 1872 found that besides an annual
sum of £79,245 devoted to " Hospital" endowments,
and £59,529 devoted to schools, there was a sum of
£35,758 which might be considered as general endowments. Of these, the best known are the Dick and
Milne Bequests, connected with the counties of
Aberdeen, Banff, and Moray. They have been used
to secure teachers qualified to give higher instruction,
and have gained a high reputation for the schools in

these counties.   By the action of the Endowments
Commission of 1882 the various endowments throughout the country had their conditions revised, and in
many cases all the educational endowments in a town
or district were amalgamated under the management
of representative trusts.   The funds are now mainly
utilized in providing bursaries or scholarships for
higher education for the children of parents of limited
income.

As regards girls, until the end of last century any
references to their education as apart from boys seem
to show that the only subjects taught to them, other
than the usual elementary branches, were sewing,
cookery, lace-work, and, in a few cases, music.   After
the beginning of the present century we find French
and drawing referred to ; but greatly as some Town
Councils interested themselves in the education of girls,
their ideas were limited to elementary and industrial
training, and it is only within very recent times that
higher instruction has been recognized as suitable, not
to say desirable, for girls.

Since 1872 Secondary Education, except that which
is provided in a number of endowed and private or
Burgh Schools proprietary schools, has been adminis-
transferred to tered by the School Boards, to whom
School Boards. the Act of that year transferred the
burgh schools from the Town Councils or other governing bodies.   The transferring clause may be considered
to describe Secondary Education as that which "does
not consist chiefly of elementary instruction in reading,

writing, and arithmetic, but of instruction in Latin, Greek, modern languages, mathematics, natural science, and generally in the higher branches of knowledge." The burgh schools giving such instruction were to be deemed higher class public schools, and to be managed by the School Boards with a view "to promote the higher education of the country," and, "so far as practicable and expedient," they were to be relieved "of the necessity of giving elementary instruction in reading, writing, and arithmetic to young children" by sufficient accommodation for elementary instruction being provided otherwise. Any endowments were transferred to the Boards, and the Town Councils were ordered to pay to the Boards from the common good the amount it had formerly been their custom to contribute to the schools. Otherwise higher education was to pay its own way. The full amount of fees was to be distributed among the masters. In other words, the schools might keep what they had, but they were to get nothing more. In six years, however, opinion had advanced far enough to allow a charge on the rates for the expense of alterations and repairs to the buildings, and, subject to the approval of the Department, such other expenses for the promotion of higher education as were not otherwise provided for. This was taken to mean that everything except salaries could now be put on the rates, and consequently the masters still depended entirely on the fees, which, with the approval of the Board, they could, by the Act of 1872, fix for themselves. The natural results were an increase in the fees charged, and the consequent exclusion of poorer children, except such as could obtain bursaries from other sources.

This state of matters continued till 1892, a year which marks an epoch in the history of secondary education in Scotland.

In the previous year the Act for assisting public elementary education in England and Wales had been passed, and in consequence Scotland became entitled to a sum equivalent to that being expended in England. As education in Scotland had already been made free from other sources, the money was available for such objects as required it.

The greater part went in relief of rates, but £30,000 was given to the universities and £60,000 was assigned

Parliamentary Grant for Secondary Education. to the Scotch Education Department for the purposes of secondary education. This is the first special grant to secondary education, and it is curious that Scotland should be indebted for it in a sense to the freeing of elementary education in England.

Committees, composed of representatives of Town or County Councils, School Boards, and other educational bodies, were formed in all the counties and larger burghs for the purpose of distributing the grant, which was allocated to them in proportion to the population and valuation of their districts. The Department are represented on every committee by one of Her Majesty's inspectors. The Committees, like the School Boards, hold office for three years. Their main function is to prepare annually a scheme for the distribution of the amount entrusted to them among the secondary schools in their district. This scheme is then submitted to the Department. As soon as it is approved, the amount allotted to a committee is paid over, and it is then the duty of the committee to distribute it to the schools in accordance with their scheme, subject to the Department having certified that the schools are in every way efficient.

In framing their schemes the committees are to have "due regard both to educational efficiency and to the **Distribution of** extension of the benefits of secondary **Secondary** education to the largest possible **Education** number of scholars"; the money is **Grant.** not to go in relief of rates. The system has now been three years in operation, and the report for the third year shows that, speaking generally, £48,000 is being distributed amongst higher class schools and State-aided schools giving higher instruction in separate secondary departments or otherwise. The money is given in the shape of direct subsidies or of capitation grants on scholars beyond the sixth standard, depending on the passes in specific subjects or the number of merit and leaving certificates gained. In most cases the grant is conditional on a number of free places being provided, and also on the reduction of fees to a moderate amount in cases where these were high. In addition to these free places some £1600 is devoted to bursaries, or scholarships, and the payment of travelling expenses of scholars requiring to go to a centre. £850 has been assigned for higher education in evening schools, and the balance has gone towards building or equipment. To this last purpose was mainly devoted a year's grant which had accumulated before the method of distribution was decided.

Opinions may differ as to the system of distribution, but there can be no doubt the grant, limited though **The Grant an** it is, has given a great impetus to **Impetus to** secondary education, and is helping **Secondary** towards better organization. The **Education.** burgh schools have been placed on a securer footing; their buildings, equipment, and staffing have been greatly improved; and they have been thrown open to a much larger number than before. New district schools have been provided; endowed and Voluntary State-aided schools have received valuable assistance; and in country districts, where no central school was possible, the schoolmasters have been encouraged to take up higher instruction, as in the old days of parish schools.

One or two of the larger School Boards have been enabled to institute special high schools for girls; but, generally speaking, the traditional "mixed" school is being continued, though greater attention is being given to subjects considered suitable for girls, and to such branches as music, painting, and drawing.

The inspection of the secondary schools in Scotland

is in the hands of the Department. In some cases

Inspection of Secondary Schools. the inspection is conducted by the ordinary inspectors; but it is more usual for special examiners, such as Professors in the Scottish Universities, to be appointed. The examiners submit a report, based on a general inspection of the school, to the Department, who then forward it to the managers. In 1886 38 secondary schools were examined in this way, 22 being higher class public schools, 10 endowed, and 6 under Voluntary managers, who invited the inspection of the Department. In 1896 the numbers were 30, 24, and 20 respectively; a total of 74 schools.

But what has come to be regarded as the real test of schools giving higher instruction is the leaving certificate

Leaving Certificate. examination, which is held annually in June. This examination arose out of a suggestion that some certificate should be associated with the inspection of higher class schools, and, after inviting the opinion of managers of secondary schools and the University authorities, it was decided that a uniform examination should be conducted for all secondary schools desiring it. The subjects of examination were English, Latin, Greek, French, German, mathematics (including arithmetic), arithmetic only, geometrical conics, analytical geometry, dynamics, and differential calculus. To these book-keeping and commercial arithmetic have since been added. Three grades of certificates are given—lower, higher, and honours. The higher is intended to correspond with the preliminary examination of the Scottish Universities, and the honours to the Indian Civil Service examination or others of the same standard. At first the examination was confined to purely secondary schools; but since 1892, when the Secondary Education grant was assigned to the Department, the higher departments of State-aided schools have been admitted, and more recently, pupil teachers. In 1888 29 secondary schools presented 972 candidates, who took 4300 papers, and gained 2334 certificates. In 1896 70 higher class schools and 259 State-aided schools presented 15,700 candidates, who took 48,000 papers, and gained nearly 20,000 certificates. Every successful candidate obtains a separate certificate for each subject in which he has passed, and these are accepted in lieu of preliminary examinations by the English and Scottish Universities, and by the medical, legal, and other professional examining bodies. At first a fee of 2s. 6d. per paper was charged to meet expenses; but except in the case of private schools, the cost is now mainly borne by the Secondary Education grant.

One noteworthy feature is that the examination is not set on prescribed work, and in this way it is hoped **Attempt to Minimise Cramming and Competition.** to prevent "cramming" for it. Also the Department do not allow one school to be compared with another, as, beyond sending the results of the examination of candidates from a particular school to the managers of that school, they do not issue any information except of a general character. Apart from this, comparison is rendered difficult by the fact that while in some schools classes are presented as a whole, in others only selected pupils are sent forward.

A general report on the way in which the papers in each subject have been worked is issued by the Secretary of the Scotch Education Department in his capacity of Director of Secondary Education. The examination is open to all schools giving higher instruction, whether public or private; and girls are admitted to it equally with boys. Its success has been such that it has almost superseded the University Local Examinations, so long the goal of secondary schools.

One other examination of recent institution deserves mention, though it will be dealt with in its proper place — the Preliminary Examination of the Scottish Universities. Such an examination existed prior to 1889; but only students desirous of taking their course in three instead of four years were required to pass it. For the last few years, however, it has been obligatory on all who wish to graduate. The absence of such an examination previously was probably due to the want of a complete system of secondary education. Since its institution it has proved of considerable service in maintaining the ideal of the schools which prepare for the universities.

The Science and Art Department has also contributed something to higher education in Scotland. Its grants have encouraged classes for science and art not only in evening schools but in many day schools. The arrangements for organized science schools have,

Work of the Science and Art Department. however, not been largely taken advantage of. Probably the difference between England and Scotland in this respect is due to the fact that in England the grant for such schools was the only grant available for higher grade schools, whereas in Scotland the payment of the ordinary Parliamentary grant on scholars up to eighteen years of age, instead of simply to the seventh standard, has given managers greater freedom, and put it in their power to provide secondary instruction even in ordinary State-aided schools.

For the same reason, probably, Scotland has few schools which can be considered strictly technical

Technical Instruction. beyond a small number of endowed institutes. The Technical Schools Act of 1887 has been almost a dead letter, and there is understood to be only one School Board which has taken advantage of it to erect a technical school. The money which fell to Town and County Councils in Scotland under the Local Taxation (Customs and Excise) Act, 1890, has not been so generally applied to education in Scotland as in England. In a number of cases the amount was too small to be of much use, and in others a fatal delay was caused by a doubt as to whether the money could be handed over except to School Boards. This doubt was finally removed only in 1892 by an amending Act.

But although nominally technical instruction makes itself little conspicuous in Scotland, in reality a great many subjects that rank elsewhere as technical are efficiently taught in day or evening schools. The Education Department are probably right in assuming, as they have done in recent Blue Books, that the Boards consider technical instruction "not so much as a separate question, but rather as one belonging to the higher sphere of education generally."

At present the Department are seeking to induce Town and County Councils to transfer the administration of funds available for education to the Secondary Education Committees described already. These funds are the residue grant of 1890, which may be applied to technical education, and a sum of £100,000 allotted by the Act of 1892, which provided the grant for secondary education. This latter sum may be used for relief of rates or for schemes of "public utility"— a term which was understood to cover education. The money, however, has already been assigned for other purposes, and it is scarcely to be hoped that much of it will be withdrawn from its present uses.

SECTION III.

ɦigber Education.

(a) UNIVERSITY EDUCATION.

THE first, and for some time the only formal recognition by the Scottish Universities of the educational needs of girls and women was the institution of the University Local Examinations, which may be said to have in some sort formed a connecting link between Secondary and Higher Education. This movement began by the admission of women to the local examinations of the University of Edinburgh, in 1865. In St. Andrews in 1864, in Glasgow in 1877, and in Aberdeen in 1880, similar examinations were organized, which from their beginning were open to girls. All these examinations were attended by greater numbers of girls than of boys.

University Local Examinations.

In all the four Universities there were three grades of examination : the preliminary or common subjects, the junior certificate, and the senior certificate. In addition to these, the University of St. Andrews instituted, in 1876, a more advanced examination (for women only) for the Diploma of L.L.A. (Lady

264

Literate in Arts); and the University of Glasgow granted, in 1879, in response to a request from the Glasgow Association for the Higher Education of Women, the Higher Local Examination for Women. All grades of the examinations were taken advantage of by girls educated in public and private schools and by home study. Special oral classes were organized in St. George's Hall, Edinburgh, classes for instruction by correspondence in Edinburgh and Glasgow, to prepare women students for them, and bursaries were offered to successful candidates. These examinations were continued in the four Universities until 1893, when they were superseded by the University Preliminary Examinations, and the leaving certificate of the Education Department (previously mentioned). The junior and senior examinations, however, are still carried on by the University of Edinburgh, and the examinations for the diploma of L.L.A. by St. Andrews.

The wish which had for some time existed in Scotland that facilities might be given to women for obtaining

Associations for the Higher Education of Women. education higher and better than that which could be acquired in their school days, and for participating to some extent in the advantages offered to men by the Universities, found voice almost simultaneously in the four University towns. St. Andrews was the first to form an Association for the Promotion of the Higher Education of Women, in 1868. This association organized courses of lectures, to be given to women by the University professors, which after a few years were discontinued on account of the small number of students attending them. The University classes were opened to women in 1892.

In Edinburgh a Ladies' Educational Association was formed in 1869, which was changed a few years later into the Association for the University Education of Women. Classes were conducted for this association by professors and lecturers, in rooms rented by its committee; and in 1874 the University of Edinburgh granted a certificate in arts to students of the association who had attended classes held by professors or lecturers whose teaching qualified for graduation, and had passed, in any three or more science or arts subjects, special examinations up to the standard of the M.A. degree. These classes were carried on until 1892, when the University arts classes were opened to women.

In Glasgow, courses of lectures to women were given by several professors of the University from 1868 onwards, but it was not until 1877 that the Glasgow Association for the Higher Education of Women was founded. Under its auspices, systematic courses were organized in University subjects (with the addition of modern languages and literatures and history), some of which were given in the University class-rooms, and others in a hall rented by the association for the purpose. These went on for six years, until, in 1883, the association was formed into a college (under the Companies' Act), to which the name of Queen Margaret College was given—in honour of Margaret, Queen of Malcolm Canmore, the first patroness of literature and art in Scotland. Two members of the Executive Council of this college were appointed by the Senate of the University, two by the School Board, and one by the Merchants' House. A year later a handsome building with extensive grounds, near the University, was provided for its work by the liberality of Mrs. John Elder. The classes were removed into this building, and from 1884 until 1892 the college course was gradually more and more assimilated to the full University curriculum for the degree of M.A. In 1889 new laboratories were built, with the result that the science classes were increased in number and completeness. In 1890 a medical school was begun with the assistance and under the direction of some of the University professors. By 1892, when the Universities were opened to women, Queen Margaret College was working on a full University curriculum in arts and medicine, besides giving some courses of lectures and practical work in science—the courses in all the faculties being, in substance and in number of lectures, the same as those given to the men students of the University.

In Aberdeen, a Ladies' Educational Association was begun in 1877. The classes instituted by it were carried on for a few years, but were not continued up till 1892, for the same reason as in St. Andrews—the difficulty in the smaller towns of obtaining a sufficient attendance of students.

In the course of the twenty years, from 1868 to 1888, repeated requests for the admission of women to degrees had been made to the Scottish Universities by the various associations for the Higher Education of Women and other bodies, but in vain, the university laws then in force rendering their admission impossible. Petitions were therefore sent up to Parliament asking that such change might be made in the laws as would legalize University education and graduation for women. In 1889 the Universities (Scotland) Act was passed, which appointed a Commission to review and, where expedient, to alter the constitution of the Scottish Universities on this and other points in which changes might be considered advisable. After other University legislation, the Commission issued an Ordinance in 1892 empowering the Universities to admit women to graduation, and to make provision within the Universities for the instruction of women in any of the subjects taught within the Universities, "either by admitting them to the ordinary" (*i.e.* hitherto attended by male students) "classes, or by instituting separate classes for their instruction as might in each case be decided by the University Court after consultation with the Senatus."

University Degrees.

On the publication of this Ordinance, the Universities of St. Andrews, Edinburgh, and Aberdeen opened their ordinary classes in science and arts to women, the teaching being entirely given in mixed classes. In Glasgow the alternative of separate classes was adopted ; and Queen Margaret College, with its buildings erected at a cost of about £24,000 and endowments of over £25,000, was transferred by its Executive Council

University Education.

and Mrs. Elder to the University, and became thenceforward the Women's Department of the University, to be governed by the University Court and Senate. Its professors and lecturers who are, in most cases, the same who teach the men students, were appointed by the Court; and the women students were admitted to graduation in arts, medicine, and science, and to all the rights and privileges of the male students, including the use of the library, museums, etc. Most of the classes for the ordinary degrees of M.A. and B.Sc., and those for the degrees of M.B., Ch.B., are held in Queen Margaret College, and for the honours degree the women students join the honours classes held in the University Lecture Rooms. A large addition was made in 1895 to the College buildings for laboratories and other rooms in connection with the medical classes, the funds for which were provided by a donation of £5000 from the Bellahouston Trust.

Thus in all the Scottish Universities graduation is now open to women on the same conditions as to men; and it is being taken full advantage of. The number of women who had graduated by September, 1896, is as follows:

	Arts.		Medicine		Science.
Edinburgh .	. 27*	...	2	...	I
Glasgow .	. 3	...	10†	...	o
St. Andrews	. 5	...	o	...	o

Aberdeen has as yet no women graduates, but on

* Four of these with honours.

† Of these, one took honours, and one passed with "high commendation."

one lady the honorary degree of LL.D. has been conferred. The difference between the number of graduates in arts in Edinburgh and Glasgow arises from the fact that in Edinburgh the. M.A. degree was made so far retrospective as to allow of its being conferred on students who had taken the pass certificates in arts instituted by that University in 1874 * in seven ˙ subjects, and to permit classes, taken by others who had been examined in at least three subjects, to count *pro tanto* towards the degree. In Glasgow the classes counted for the degree date from 1892 ; and most of the students preparing for the M.A. are working for honours, and taking a four or five years' course. On the other hand, in Glasgow the classes of the School of Medicine for Women, having been from the first organized for the purpose of preparation for the University degree, were at once recognized (in 1892) by the University Court as classes qualifying for the degree, whereas the recognition of the Edinburgh classes took place two years later.

The number of women students attending the classes in the Scottish Universities in session 1895-6 was as follows :

	Arts.	Medicine.	Science.	Music.
Aberdeen	34	I	—	—
St. Andrews	37	—	—	—
Edinburgh	160	—	2	' 5
Glasgow	167	72	3	—

In Edinburgh there were also 39 studying medicine

---

* See page 266.

in extra-mural classes, with a view to graduation, and 35 non-matriculated women studying music only.

The Ordinances of the Universities Commissioners, which came into force in 1892, introduced considerable **Regulations for** changes into the regulations for the **University** degrees. In accordance with the new **Examinations.** regulations all students entering for a degree in arts have to take a preliminary examination in (*a*) English, (*b*) Latin or Greek, (*c*) mathematics, (*d*) one of the following : Latin or Greek (if not already taken), French, German, Italian, dynamics. After this has been passed, attendance on University classes for at least three winters, or two winters and three summers, is required (longer time may be taken if wished) ; and the student must take classes in, and be examined in, seven subjects for the ordinary degree, or five for the honours degree, at least two of these being on a considerably higher standard than for the ordinary degree. Science students have the same preliminary examination as that required for arts, except that French or German may be substituted for Latin or Greek, and that mathematics must be passed on the higher standard. For the B.Sc. degree not less than three years' study in the University is requisite, including four full courses of higher instruction and practical or laboratory work, besides three subjects taken on the same standard as that of the ordinary degree of M.A. The degree of D.Sc. can be taken five years after that of B.Sc., and each candidate has to present a thesis or published memoir of work, to be approved by the Senate of the University. For medical students the preliminary examination includes (*a*) English, (*b*) Latin, (*c*) elementary mathematics, and (*d*) Greek or French or German; and the papers are on a somewhat lower standard than those of the preliminary examination for the arts and science degrees. A candidate must, after passing the preliminary examination, be engaged in medical study for at least five years before the degree of M.B., Ch.B. can be conferred, and two years more, and additional examinations, are required for the degrees of M.D. and M.S.

All matriculated women students have votes in the election of the Lord Rector of the University they attend; and women graduates become, by the fact of their graduation, members of the General Council of their University.

During their years of study, women students may **Halls of** take advantage of the accommodation **Residence for** offered by the halls of residence **Women Students.** which have been opened for their benefit in Glasgow, Edinburgh, and St. Andrews, but they are free to live at home or in lodgings if they prefer it.

University Extension lectures are given in various parts of Scotland in connection with the Universities of **University** Edinburgh and Glasgow. The volun-**Extension** tary examinations which may be held **Lectures.** by the lecturers do not count in any way towards University graduation. These classes were organized chiefly with a view to "meeting the wants of (1) ladies, (2) clerks and other persons engaged in business, and (3) artisans of all classes."

Classes for instruction by correspondence were begun in Edinburgh in 1876, and in Glasgow in 1878, to

Correspondence Classes. prepare candidates for the local examinations of the Universities, and to assist in general private study persons who are unable to attend oral classes. The Edinburgh correspondence classes now prepare for the Edinburgh local examinations, the preliminary examinations of the Scottish Universities, and the LL. A. examinations of St. Andrews; those of Glasgow prepare for the preliminary examinations of the Scottish Universities, the matriculation examination of London University, and the Cambridge junior, senior, and higher local examinations. Additional classes in literature, languages, science, and art are formed for students who do not propose to take any University examination.

Technical and Professional Education

PROVISION is made for the scientific education of women, as has been seen above, by their admission

Science. to the science classes and laboratory work in the Universities. They are also admitted to the science classes in the Glasgow and West of Scotland Technical College, and to the Heriot-Watt College in Edinburgh. They thus prepare themselves for teaching science subjects, or for posts in laboratories, business, or works where a knowledge of natural science is required.

Towards the education of women for the profession of medicine the first steps were taken in 1869, when

Medicine. Miss Jex-Blake, Mrs. Thorne, Miss Pechey, Mrs. Evans, and Miss Chaplin came to Edinburgh and applied for admission to medical classes in the University. They were allowed to matriculate, and to register as medical students ; but with regard to their medical course of instruction many difficulties were made. Permission was given at first that they should be taught in classes separate from those of the men, with the proviso that although the

medical professors should be allowed to give such
classes, no professor should be compelled to do so.
For the first two years they obtained the necessary
instruction, partly within the University and partly in
extra-mural classes; but the difficulty of procuring
the teaching and clinical work required for the last
two years of the curriculum was so great that the
ladies had recourse to an action in the Scottish Law
Courts to oblige the University to give them such
facilities as would enable them to complete their
medical education and proceed to take the degree.
The legal decision was against them in 1873, though
by a very small majority of the judges. The ladies
then went to London, and, with the co-operation of
others, founded the London School of Medicine for
Women, in 1874. Twelve years later, when, in 1886,
the conjoint Colleges of Physicians and Surgeons of
Edinburgh and Glasgow agreed to admit women to
their diplomas (sometimes called the "triple qualification"), Dr. Jex-Blake, who had meantime taken the
degree of M.D., Berne, and a diploma from the Irish
College of Surgeons, returned to Edinburgh, and
founded there the Edinburgh School of Medicine
for Women, in Surgeon Square. At first this school
prepared most of its students for the diploma of the
conjoint Colleges of Physicians and Surgeons of
Edinburgh and Glasgow, as did also the Medical
College for Women, Chambers Street, Edinburgh, a
second school of medicine, founded in 1889. In
1894 the University of Edinburgh recognized the

classes of both these institutions, which belong to the Extra-Mural School of Medicine in Edinburgh, but are not part of the University, nor directly under its government, as qualifying for its examinations and degrees. Women are not, however, admitted in Edinburgh to the classes of the University professors in the Medical Faculty, as they are in those of the Arts Faculty. The students of both the above schools have facilities for clinical work in the Royal Infirmary, Edinburgh.

In Glasgow the Medical School for Women, which was, as previously mentioned, added to Queen Margaret College in 1890, passed with the College into the University of Glasgow in 1892, and from that date formed the medical department for women of that University preparing students for the University examinations and degrees. The foundation of this school was made easy by the generosity of Mrs. John Elder, donor of the college buildings, who met the initial expenses of the first two years of its existence; and by the most kind and ready help of the professors of the University, some of whom, notably Professor Young, devoted much time and trouble to its organization and improvement. Several of the · professors lecture in the school, the rest of the staff being appointed by the University Court. The students have the advantage of frequently seeing experiments and illustrations of the teaching given by means of the University apparatus and collections in several departments, *e.g.* in Professor McKendrick's physiology classes and in natural history. Clinical and dispensary instruction is given in the Glasgow Royal Infirmary, where wards are reserved for the instruction of women, the Royal Hospital for Sick Children, the Glasgow Maternity and other hospitals for special diseases, including the treatment of the eye, insanity, fevers, etc.

In Aberdeen and St. Andrews women are admitted to the University medical classes for men ; also to the men's classes in Dundee University College, which is affiliated to St. Andrews. But as St. Andrews and Dundee give only part of the medical curriculum, no provision being made by them for the two last years of the course, both men and women students have to take the last part of their work elsewhere, in any University or medical school they may select.

For the profession of nursing, women can be fully trained in the Royal Infirmary, Edinburgh, and in the Royal and Western Infirmaries, **Nursing.** Glasgow, in two training homes for nurses in Glasgow, and in various other hospitals in Scotland. Special training is given for maternity nursing in the Maternity Hospitals in Edinburgh and Glasgow, and for missionary nursing, in a training home for the purpose, at Westercraigs, Glasgow. Special preparation is given for mission work, independent of nursing, in the Training Institution for Mission Workers, Burnbank Terrace, Glasgow, and other institutions.

Training for teaching in schools is provided in the normal colleges in connection with the Established **Training of** and Free Churches of Scotland in **Teachers.** Edinburgh, Glasgow, and Aberdeen ;

in the Episcopal Training College in Edinburgh, and the Roman Catholic Training College in Glasgow. Through the Government Education Department a certain number of "Queen's scholarships" are offered, which are open to men and women who are entering the normal colleges. An opening has recently been given by the Department for some "Queen's student-ships," which will provide University education for women teachers who have been educated in public schools, but have not taken the Normal College course of instruction. The scheme for these, however, has not yet been fully completed. The Universities give courses of lectures on education. In Edinburgh, St. George's Training College prepares secondary teachers for their work in schools or families, and for the examination for the teachers' certificates of London and Cambridge.

In Art, women have the same opportunities for study as men, all the Schools of Art being open to them, including the Government Schools in Edinburgh, Glasgow, and nine other towns, besides several Schools of Art conducted under other auspices. Government examinations in Art are held yearly, and the scholarships and prizes are open to women as to men.

Art.

Edinburgh is the only one of the Scottish Universities which has a Chair of Music ; the classes and degree given in connection with it are open to women. Examinations in Music are held yearly in the large towns by the Associated

Music.

Board of the Royal Academy and Royal College of Music; also by Trinity College, London.

In cookery, training is given by the Schools of Cookery in Edinburgh and Glasgow; also instruction

Domestic Economy. in laundry work, needlework, dressmaking, millinery, and other subjects of Domestic Economy; teachers are prepared for giving lessons in these branches, and for taking the examinations for the diplomas and certificates of the National Union for the Technical Education of Women in Domestic Sciences.

Instruction is also available in typewriting, shorthand,

For Business. book-keeping, etc., for women who wish to enter on work in offices or houses of business.

It will be seen from the facts given above that the days of inferior educational advantages and facilities for study given to women in comparison with those offered to men are in Scotland a thing of the past. From the Infant School up to the Honours Classes and Degrees of the Universities, all possibilities of education are open to them, in most cases by means of mixed classes, and in others by special classes. Women have thus as good opportunities now for preparing themselves for professional or other work as those which are available for men.

APPENDIX I.

THE PROFESSIONAL ORGANIZATIONS OF TEACHERS

TEACHERS have been the latest of the professions to organize themselves into trade or professional unions. The work has proceeded rapidly, so that before many years are over we may expect an unattached teacher to be quite rare. The College of Preceptors has the honour of being the oldest body which recognized the need of raising the teachers' status by means of combination. In the matter of teachers' registration, the College has always advocated a separate register for secondary teachers, a policy which has tended to defer the passing of a Teachers Registration Bill. The Teachers' Guild, on the other hand, advocates a single register, including both Elementary and Secondary School Teachers. The teaching profession cannot now be strictly termed unorganized. The initiative has proceeded from the members themselves, a fact of great significance, which cannot fail to secure greater play for the individuality of the teacher when the time, now rapidly approaching, will allow of the State organization of Secondary Education. The uniforming influence of the Code and allocation of Government Grant have assisted the remarkable development of the National Union of Teachers, founded in 1870. The accompanying tables may help to show how organization is the order of the day in every branch of the teaching profession. In the organizations of Elementary School Teachers women lag behind men in numbers. This is not the case with secondary teachers ; organized women outnumber the men.

Title.	Date of Foundation.	No. and Sex of Members.	Annual Subscription.	Benevolent Fund.	Aims.
1. National Union of Teachers.	1870	33,000, mixed.	7s. to centre, plus local fee.	£65,000; orphanage, sick and superannuation fund.	To watch the working of the Code; communicate with the Education Department; obtain pensions for teachers; establish provident, benevolent, and orphanage funds; secure Parliamentary representation; provide legal advice.
2. Metropolitan Board Teachers' Association.	1872	6000, mixed.	3s. 6d.	Mutual insurance fund; 2000 members each pay 1s. on death of member.	To ascertain, represent, and support opinions of teachers under the London School Board.
3. National Association of Voluntary Teachers.	1888	(no returns), mixed.	Head Teachers, 2s. 3d.; others, 1s. 3d.	Shilling Mutual Insurance Fund.	Seeks to obtain increased imperial aid for Voluntary Schools; to ascertain, represent, and support opinions of members; approves superannuation scheme; desires definite religious instruction.
4. National Federation of Assistant Teachers.	1892	5507, mixed.	1s. to 2s. 6d.	None.	Seeks the redress of special grievances; works heartily with N.U.T. (1).
5. Association of Head-masters of Higher Grade and Organized Science Schools*	1892	80, men.	21s.	None.	Purely educational aims; confers with other educational bodies; desires wise and just expenditure of public money; concerns itself with organization and methods, but not personal matters and relations.

* Might be classed equally well with Secondary Associations.

B.—ASSOCIATIONS OF SECONDARY TEACHERS.

Title.	Date of Foundation.	No. and Sex of Members.	Annual Subscription.	Benevolent Fund.	Aims.
1. College of Preceptors.	1846	1100, mixed.	Guinea.	£2300.	"To promote sound learning, advance interests of education. . . . Give facilities to teacher for acquiring knowledge of his profession." Grants teachers' diplomas, and scholars' certificates, &c.; handsome members' rooms, and lecture hall.
2. Head-masters' Conference.	1871	90, men.	No information.		To enable head-masters of first-grade schools to meet together and discuss matters of interest to them.
3. Association of Head-mistresses.	1874	147, women.	£1.	Nucleus just forming.	To confer on such matters as concern secondary education, and take action when necessary.
4. The Teachers' Guild.	1883	4300, mixed, two-thirds women.	6s. 6d. to 7s. 6d.	No fund ; thrift encouraged in various ways.	To represent all grades of teachers, obtain for them the status of a learned profession, and advance their welfare generally.
5. University Association of Women Teachers.	1883	579, women.	5s.	None.	To promote common interests ; provide lectures, teachers, examiners.

Title.	Date of Foundation.	No. and Sex of Members.	Annual Subscription.	Benevolent Fund.	Aims.
6. Private Schools' Association.	1883	701, mixed.	10s. 6d.	None.	To protect the interests of private schools; resist unjust legislation; recover debts; discussion.
7. Association of Assistant Mistresses.	1884	565, women.	2s. 6d.	None.	Discussion of educational questions; improvement of hours, salaries, &c., of members.
8. Incorporated Association of Head-masters.	1890	319, men.	10s.	(Under consideration).	Discussion and interchange of ideas; to influence public bodies connected with education; watch and suggest legislation.
9. Assistant Masters' Association.	1891	602, men.	4s.	None at present.	To promote and watch over interests of members; has agency department.
10. Association of the Head-masters of Preparatory Schools.	1892	148, men.	10s.	Beginning one, but for assistant masters only.	To organize members' opinions; advance interests; provide a channel of communication with educational bodies.

Appendix II.

"FREE" EDUCATION

It has been suggested that an analysis of the cost of Elementary Education might prove useful to those who do not quite grasp the rather complicated figures whose totality equals the annual cost of a child's education in the Board and Voluntary Schools. "Free" education is the result of an additional subsidy paid by the State out of the imperial taxation. Every man, woman, and child contributes to imperial taxation, so that now the greater share of a child's education is paid by the community at large. In the case of a child in a Board School, the next largest contribution is made by the locality in which such child resides. It is evident that the ratepayers are a larger class than the parents. A "free" library is usually maintained by the ratepayers. Their share in the payment of a child's education is two-fifths of the whole—£1 out of £2 10s., in round numbers. With insignificant exceptions, Elementary Schools have been free since the Free Education Act of 1891 came into operation, *i.e.* September, 1892. The additional contribution by the State, which replaces school fees, equals 10s. per child, and is technically known as the fee-grant.

In the text of this book stress has been laid on the fact that Voluntary Schools receive no aid from the rates; their managers usually object to control by the ratepayers. Voluntary Schools have also accepted the fee-grant; as a matter of fact, only 114 schools, out of a total of nearly 20,000, have refused it, though many Voluntary Schools charge fees for the majority of their scholars, and only accept the fee-grant for a certain number. Voluntary

284

Schools must therefore find the £1 per scholar which Board Schools obtain from the rates, or part of the £1, from some other source. This they do by subscriptions from those who sufficiently desire denominational religious teaching to pay for it, by endowment, and in some schools by fees. The rates are a far more steady and certain source of revenue than subscriptions, which do not increase at the same rate as the children. Thus, although subscriptions had slightly increased in 1895, per head they worked out to 6s. 8¾d., as against 6s. 10d. in 1891. The following tables have been simplified to make the analysis of cost more easy to comprehend :—

			£	s.	d.
A.	Cost of child's education in Board School .	.	2	10	8
B.	,, ,, Voluntary School .		1	19	0

A. *Analysis of Cost of Board School Child's Education.*

	£	s.	d.	
From the Government Grant * .	0	18	8½	} Paid by
,, Fee-grant . .	0	10	0	} the State.
,, Rates . . .	1	0	0	
Various sources (about) . .	0	1	11½	
	£2	10	8	

B. *Analysis of Cost of Voluntary School Child's Education.*

	£	s.	d.	
Government Grant . .	0	18	0	} Paid by
Fee-grant . . .	0	10	0	} the State.
Subscriptions . .	0	6	8¾	
School fees . .	0	2	0	.
Endowment and various . .	0	2	3½	
	£1	19	0	

Before the introduction of free education the analysis of the cost of education worked out as follows :—

1891.

			£	s.	d.
A.	Cost of child's education in Board School .	.	2	7	8
B.	,, ,, Voluntary School .		1	17	9

* The figure given in the Report for the Committee of Council, 1895–96, 19s. 5d., may be called an estimate. The increased attendance of that year caused the grant to work out to 18s. 8½d. The figures are here very slightly manipulated.

Analysis of A.

	£	s.	d.
Government Grant . .	0	18	9½
Rates	0	19	3½
Board School fees . . .	0	9	1¾
Various	0	0	5¼
	£2	7	8

Analysis of B.

	£	s.	d.
Government Grant . .	0	18	0
Subscriptions . . .	0	6	10
Voluntary School fees . .	0	11	4¾
Endowment and various . .	0	1	6¼
	£1	17	9

It must be understood that these figures refer to "maintenance" only. A further difference exists between Board and Voluntary Schools, in that the former are built out of the ratepayers' money, save in cases where managers have transferred Voluntary Schools to School Boards; whereas Voluntary Schools have usually been erected at the cost of the different religious denominations. For the most part, Voluntary School buildings are older, less convenient, and less adapted for teaching purposes than Board Schools.

On the whole it is probable that there exists less desire on the part of the general public to maintain Voluntary Schools than used to be the case. The fact that subscriptions are diminishing per head (of the children), and that in many cases the Voluntary Schools have suffered by accepting the 10s. fee-grant in lieu of fees, adds to the financial difficulties of managers. Whether the fee-grant is profit or loss to School Boards and managers is largely a question of North *versus* South, town against country. North and town have lost, South and country gained by accepting the additional fixed contribution of the State.

INDEX

Aberdare Hall: 152
Aberystwyth College: 97, 150-1
Academies, Rise of, in Scotland: 252-3
Acland, Rt. Hon. A. H. D.: 61, 201; Motion of, 202
Acts, Education: Difference between English and Scottish, 238-9
— Schism: Passing of, 22
— Technical Instruction: Passing of, 201
Addison, Joseph: 10
Adult Education, Secondary: 107
Affiliation Scheme: 160
Alexandra Hall: Opening of, 151
Alford, Dean: 74
Ambleside, House of Education: 176
Anderson, Mrs. Garrett: 107, 178
Anstie, Dr.: 178
Argyll, Duke of: Speech of, 20
Armitage-Smith, Mr. G.: 209; Report of, 125-6
Art, Schools of: Number of, 106; Scottish, 278
Assistant Masters' Association: 284; Mistresses' Association, 284
Association for Education of Women, Oxford: 138
— for Home Arts and Industries: 214-5
— Incorporated, of Head-Masters: 283

Association of Assistant Masters: 284; Mistresses, 284
— of Head-Masters of Higher Grade and Organized Science Schools: 282; Preparatory Schools, 284
— of Head-Mistresses: 283
—Metropolitan Board Teachers': 282
—Voluntary Teachers, National: 282
— Private Schools': 284
— University, of Women Teachers: 283
Associations, Educational, of Women: Rise of, 130
— for Higher Education of Women (Scottish): 265-6, 267-8
Astell, Mary: Complaint of, 9; Efforts for better Education, 124
Attendance, Compulsory, in England: 44; Scotland, 239

Bangor College: 150
Bartley, Mr. G. C. T.: 23
Beale, Miss: 76, 116, 117, 173
Bedford College: 76; Unique Position of, 129-30
Bell, Dr. Andrew: 14, 26, 28, 29, 164
Bellahouston Trust, The: 269
Bethnal Green National Schools: 34
Bills, Educational: 30

PLYMOUTH

WILLIAM BRENDON AND SON, PRINTERS.

1

www.ingramcontent.com/pod-product-compliance
Lightning Source LLC
Chambersburg PA
CBHW031359270326
41929CB00010BA/1244